Behavioral Management in the Public Schools

Behavioral Management in the Public Schools

An Urban Approach

Edited by
Nancy R. Macciomei and Douglas H. Ruben

Westport, Connecticut
London

Library of Congress Cataloging-in-Publication Data

Behavioral management in the public schools : an urban approach /
   edited by Nancy R. Macciomei, Douglas H. Ruben.
       p.   cm.
   Includes bibliographical references (p.   ) and index.
   ISBN 0–275–96327–6 (alk. paper)
   1. Behavior modification—United States.   2. Public schools—
Social aspects—United States.   3. Problem children—Behavior
modification—United States.   4. Education, Urban—United States.
   I. Macciomei, Nancy R.   II. Ruben, Douglas H.
LB1060.2.B44   1999
371.39'3'0973—dc21   99–21600

British Library Cataloguing in Publication Data is available.

Library of Congress Catalog Card Number: 99–21600
ISBN: 0–275–96327–6

First published in 1999

Praeger Publishers, 88 Post Road West, Westport, CT 06881
An imprint of Greenwood Publishing Group, Inc.
www.praeger.com

Printed in the United States of America

The paper used in this book complies with the
Permanent Paper Standard issued by the National
Information Standards Organization (Z39.48–1984).

10 9 8 7 6 5 4 3 2 1

Contents

Preface   vii

Part I   Problems in Urban Schoolchild Discipline   1

1 Behavior Problems in Urban Schoolchildren   3
   Nancy R. Macciomei

2 Why Traditional Behavior Modification Fails with Urban Children   19
   Douglas H. Ruben

Part II   Current Advances in Urban Behavioral Management   39

3 Alternative Systems for Assessment and Grading Students   41
   Nancy R. Macciomei

4 Computer Technology for High-Risk Students   53
   Nancy R. Macciomei and Gregg Byrum

5 Cultural Diversity in the Classroom   71
   Nancy R. Macciomei

6 Effective Approaches for Schoolwide and Classroom Behavior
   Management   85
   Nancy R. Macciomei

7 Peer Mediation and Positive Discipline with Hard-to-Reach
   Students   101
   Jim Ciociola

8   Community-Based Instruction and Experiences in Building
    Self-Esteem   111
    Suzanne S. Piazzola

9   Teaching Students with Serious Emotional and Behavioral
    Problems: A Teacher's Perspective   127
    Barry G. Macciomei

References   143

Index   155

About the Editors and Contributors   161

Preface

Nearly half a century ago the paralyzing educational problems of urbanized students were well documented. These problems existed for a variety of reasons. Poverty, street gangs, and poor educational expectations plagued inner-city, underprivileged students in many discriminatory ways. Racial tensions sparked classroom unrest and cast a shadow of distrust among teachers and students. Inequities between working class and middle class grew more divisive and propelled ethnic, religious, and political prejudices, stereotyping the socially undesirable. Fears of communism infected youthful minds, further proliferating views that the world was unsafe and that threats of inland invasions were imminent. Believers of Armageddon harbored hatred and dispassion and felt their only offense against a cruel society was self-preservation. They built fallout shelters, radically protested against the government, and condoned their school-age children's unmerciful teasing of suspicious classmates.

Urban life in the 1950s clearly had its own turmoil. Untempered social hostilities built on suspicion created a precarious life for inner-city neighborhood students. Their anger and distrust were nebulous, not specific. Targets of malicious or aggressive acts simply were the surrogates for bigger, more intangible problems that could not be confronted.

Proliferation of distrust, anguish, and fear of domination powerfully fueled urban decay 50 years ago. Fear mobilized a delusion that some students were good, and some were bad. Some students held patriotic, devout Christian values self-perceived as superior, while other students randomly labeled as outsiders were vilified and segregated from mainstream school activities. Animosity channeled its way malignantly through peer interactions and teacher–student relationships. An undercurrent of conspicuously heated tension filled the classrooms and spread like a virus onto playgrounds and athletic fields.

But anger never turned uncontrollably and unpredictably violent. Belligerent feelings used to, and still do, explode in harsh verbal exchanges, fistfights, and even threats of vengeance, the latter of which rarely were carried out. Students hurt each other, but they did not kill each other; acts of aggression rarely were arbitrary and capricious.

That is contrary to today's shocking headlines of random school-ground shootings, stabbings, beatings, and bewildering carnage. Many urban schools no longer are breeding grounds for suspicion; they are war zones. Rapidly emerging in inner-city as well as suburban classrooms is a jungle mentality of survival of the fittest. Weak subversives who are academically conscious are literally outnumbered by street-smart gang members dominant in force and weaponry. Accessibility to firearms from illegal purchases or liberally minded, gun-collecting parents produces a growing arsenal contributing to youth crimes. Murderers under 15 years of age constitute a staggering statistic of school-age arrests related to homicide and robbery. Teenage gunmen, for example, riddled a playground of children 13 to 18 years old in San Francisco's Chinatown. In Richmond, Virginia, a 14-year-old opened fire on a coach and teaching aide during a shooting spree following gang-related arguments. From February 1997, until May 1999, eight school shootings erupted unexpectedly in elementary and high schools, leaving several children seriously wounded or fatally shot. From Alaska to Colorado to Georgia, firearm crimes by juveniles reached epidemic proportions and completely shattered the tradition of school as a safe paradise for learning.

Current urban school shootings are disastrously destroying the sanctity of education. Harmless name-calling and fistfights during the 1950s incredibly have advanced into homicidal acts of prepubescent vengeance. Distraught youngsters betrayed or devastated by their peers now are self-proclaimed vigilantes. They regain their honor by killing instead of slicing tires or toilet-papering household shrubs. Fayetteville, Tennessee, 18-year-old Jacob Davis exemplifies this contagious pathology. Despondent over his girlfriend's dating another guy, he hunted down and fatally shot his rival, Robert "Nick" Creson, as Creson entered the school parking lot. And why? Because the Fayetteville youth, consumed with jealousy, did not know what else to do.

This is precisely why *Behavioral Management in the Public Schools: An Urban Approach* came about. Urbanity poses uniquely complex and demanding behavior problems exhibited in school-age children. While always a challenge for educators, urban students now represent more than a challenge. They are unknowing perpetrators of a deadly trend in impulsive and psychopathic crimes that completely rewrite the moral codes of conduct and force educators to revise enforceable interventions. The disheartening exigencies of modern, inner-city schools sadly warrant a fresh start at old questions, Why do kids get in trouble? What should teachers do about it?

This book responds to these innocent questions with a ready prescription for teachers at their wit's end. The book introduces effectively proven strategies to assess and manage at-risk behaviors while promoting healthy adolescent self-esteem. Besides teenage shooters, concerns also arise regarding high truancy rates, low test scores, fears of student safety, and, consequently, minimal instruction due to continuous classroom disruption. Traditional programming once solved many of these headaches. Now it does not. Discipline interventions are old-fashioned, recycled versions of strategies used with low-risk populations and, more dangerously, are predicated on untenable theories about the causality of behavior.

A fistfight in gym, for example, now goes beyond a garden-variety case of improper behavior punishable by suspension or moralistic discussion with the assistant principal. Antiquated methods are replaced by innovations directly linked to practical, everyday issues such as (1) is this an abused or neglected child who knows only how to fight to survive?; (2) is fighting the only mode of communication this child knows to express feelings?; and (3) is removal of fighting achievable through such options as problem solving and peer mediation?

The brutal reality underlying revisions of school management techniques is this: traditional interventions relied on methods that were presumed effective and based on scientific principles of behavior change. But the kids are different, and environments they operate in are different. Even if the principles of behavior change are scientific, the variables of environment and lifestyles remain untested empirically and thus limit standard procedures used in the past. Such limits may now mitigate or preclude old procedures and warrant new procedures involving the new variables of environment and lifestyles.

Qualifying variables relative to high-risk, urban behavior is the subject of each chapter. The book is therefore divided into two parts covering etiological and classroom strategy issues. Part I is on "Problems in Urban Schoolchild Discipline" and overviews recurrent problems observed in urban students against a backdrop of ineffective strategies. Changes in methodology optimistically adopt a realistic perspective on student delinquency and indicate a shift in discipline philosophy.

Part II is on "Current Advances in Urban Behavioral Management." Intimately explored are teacher-tested, effective methods used on behaviorally disruptive students from kindergarten to high school. Chapters are technically explicit as well as informative on problems of cultural diversity, sustaining motivation, and collateral effects of instructional decay on student learning. Incentive-based strategies employ startling, creative uses of computers, classroom monitoring, and curricula assessment rarely visible in urban school settings. Peer-mediation procedures, in particular, borrow from concepts of participative management and a self-regulatory workforce. Students under peer monitoring are increasingly prone to class conformity and improve in self-paced work.

But let the truth be spoken. Managing high-risk students may not be appealing to many educators. After all, teaching is a two-way street, reciprocally involving eager learners and motivated instructors. Knowing this, the editors offer a word of empathy: educators who work with urban children and parents discover intrinsic rewards in reaching successful goals. Inherent rewards may be neither as immediate nor as obvious as instructors would like them to be. That is why the goals have to be different. Goals that seek *to teach students with minimal interruption and maximal skill learning are goals worth pursuing.* Teachers and administrators who accept this alternate thinking will succeed in instructing children and making urban obstacles another unit in the total school curriculum.

PART I

PROBLEMS IN URBAN
SCHOOLCHILD DISCIPLINE

Behavior Problems in Urban Schoolchildren

Nancy R. Macciomei

Emotional and behavioral problems of school-aged children in the classroom rank as the number one concern of educators, administrators, and the general public. There have been significant activities in the development and implementation of programs as well as the reauthorization of laws that qualify for exceptional programming. However, most students do not qualify for special programming. They continue to disrupt learning for themselves and for others; their intensity, frequency, and duration of inappropriate behaviors create an unsafe and disorderly environment. Across the nation, schools in the urban areas have problems that seem to be more extensive and intensive than ever before.

Most public schools try to educate all students utilizing traditional activities and instructional methods. However, the most complex and demanding task of all educators who work with students exhibiting serious problem behaviors is day-to-day classroom behavior management. Pupils who are chronically disruptive, defiant, withdrawn, or aggressive possess minimal social or functional communication. Such deficiencies often are difficult to handle even in one-to-one situations. Traditional classroom behavior management is possible but not always reliable. Management of pupil behavior in group settings, organizing the curriculum, arranging and individualizing instruction, and evaluating students' learning all constitute current methods (Kerr & Nelson, 1998).

The recurrent difficulty lies not with methodology per se, but with *social validity*. Procedures ideally prescribed for classroom management simply do not fit the urban child's repertoire of oppositional behavior. This chapter introduces the wide range of malcontents typically encountered in urban classrooms and overviews reasons for defective behavioral programming. First reviewed is the urban ambience of the classroom. Second, failures of past discipline are considered. Third examined are underlying causes of discipline problems related to teacher–student and systemic school intervention. Fourth, routine behavior disturbances are explored. Fifth, factors influencing lack of school control are noted. Finally provided are a rationale and purpose for teaching self-control to high-risk students.

THE URBAN ENVIRONMENT

A city or urban setting reflects a place where populations tend to cluster into neighborhoods on the basis of related social characteristics. Common social characteristics might include amounts of education, lifestyle, stage in life cycle, occupation, religion, or race. American cities have become a collection of diverse groups reflecting differing values. To some, the values contrast with their own. To others, certain values are viewed as oppositional. Within the urban setting, ethnic and social differences are combined to create a true melting-pot society.

Urbanization includes a variety of distinct and intense interests and attitudes that create a variety of social problems. Urban social problems are the dilemma of sizable numbers of people gathered together to live and function within the city limits. Many parts of urban America live in cities that were once blossoming and now are slowly deteriorating. The neighborhoods surrounding many cities are also characterized by high crime rates and low socioeconomic status, with as many as 80% or more of school-age children receiving free or reduced lunches (Beck & Gabriel, 1990). Bound by poverty and unemployment, the ghetto population and working poor live out lives devoid of the niceties that other Americans may enjoy. These characteristics have significant implication for social problems that manifest both at home and in the classroom.

The number of children with behavior and emotional problems living in urban areas (population over 60,000) has risen within the last five years. Conservative estimates suggest that 15% of all children in metropolitan areas would be considered highrisk children (Wood et al., 1985). However, only one-tenth to one-third of these children are receiving minimal, if any, services to alter behaviors. The wide range of childhood emotional and behavioral dysfunctions may be factors brought on by living in these stressful conditions. Vulnerability and environmental stressors may disrupt a child's capacity to achieve acceptable coping and social behaviors. Disruptive behaviors in the classroom are likely to have been created by a mixture of familial, societal, and individual hardship factors.

The behaviors demonstrated in classrooms each day reflect a limited capacity to problem-solve, observe, reflect, and use self-control and self-management. Common behavior problems stem from a lack of impulse control (Carr et al., 1994) The urban child demonstrates high degrees of aggressive behavior, a limited capacity to cooperate, and a lack of control with self-direction. Children living in these conditions are considered high-risk for problematic behaviors and emotional problems. The results are evidenced by disillusionment and antagonism toward traditional educational practices and defiance toward authority figures. Secondary results are negative self-concepts and general underdevelopment of skills for coping with life's problems. Other effects are high delinquency and dropout rates, gross limitations in basic learning skills, and excessive misbehavior in the classroom. There is also evidence that urban children have learned to adapt to harsh or unstable circumstances by means of impulsive, unstable, and often explosive actions in their community.

Most of society, which controls pathways to economic, social, political, and personal success, demands higher levels of self-control and forethought. Unfortunately for our city children, these levels are not readily attainable by urban school-age children who find the action-impulse mode appropriate for their everyday existence.

Student's Response to Urban Inequities

Urban schoolchildren are currently demonstrating high levels of frustration and impulsiveness. This is largely because of their increased awareness of social inequities. Students' frustration, anger, and hostility respond to a single realization: they have been victims of a negative environment, a realization that may then trigger emotional energies that are not being dealt with effectively inside the urban school. Braaten (1987) agrees that educators need effective, nontraditional motivational and behavioral management programs that will help urban children do things well, gaining control over their own lives.

Implementing such programs in large school systems is often difficult and not done on a consistent or extended basis. If presented over a long, consistent period, the interventions within the next chapters may be productive in helping children retain the education that they need. The biggest challenge we face as educators is stepping outside our own cultural orientation so that we can develop a greater appreciation for, and understanding of, those who are different. We must be able to utilize and depend on nontraditional teaching techniques that reflect our commitment to educate all students.

DISCIPLINE IN THE PAST

Discipline has always been connected with a goal or purpose. Individual discipline is often thought of as organizing one's impulses to attain a goal; group discipline demands control of impulses of the individuals in a group to attain an accepted goal. Throughout most of American education, fear of corporal punishment was a major instrument of student discipline. Infliction of physical pain was justified on the same grounds as were the harsh penal codes for adults. Wood et al. (1985) concur that this was considered a humiliating disciplinary system. The American colonists, coming from a land where flogging was common in schools, took it for granted that corporal punishment should be used to control the children in the schools they established in the New World.

In the recent past, in making a decision about punishing a student, an administrator generally chose among the following options:

- Verbal punishment ("chewing out")
- Detention (student stays after school)

- Assigned work around the building
- Suspension
- Expulsion
- Corporal punishment

Corporal Punishment

While the use of corporal punishment in the schools may be legal if state law and school board policy permit it, there continues to be considerable disagreement on the part of teachers, parents, and educational authorities about its desirability and effectiveness. Supporters of corporal punishment argue that nothing else has worked with some students and that some students respond only to physical punishment. This is usually because students experience punishment at home. Supporters also debate that physical punishment is effective because it makes the student think twice before committing the same offense and is a deterrent to other students who might break a similar rule (Horner et al., 1994).

Opponents harshly take issue with these traditional viewpoints. Lobbying against punishment, regardless of what the Supreme Court rules, many professionals claim corporal punishment is cruel and inhumane. Also, corporal punishment holds considerable potential for child abuse. Lastly, Gorton (1983) states that there are more effective, nonphysical alternatives to correcting students' misbehavior. Although surveys have shown that more than two-thirds of the states authorize school districts to utilize corporal punishment in the schools, no school district in America is required to have corporal punishment as policy.

Boonin (1979) recommends that educational authorities consider the following guidelines, extracted from various court decisions and recommended by education authorities:

1. Corporal punishment should not be used at all except when the acts of misconduct are so antisocial in nature or so shocking to the conscience that extreme punishment seems warranted.

2. The particular offenses that will result in corporal punishment should be specified. Also, the nature of the corporal punishment that will be permitted should be made explicit.

3. Evidence that other, nonphysical methods were used earlier in an attempt to help the student improve his or her behavior should be required before corporal punishment is employed.

4. Corporal punishment should not be used in situations where physical restraint is more properly called for. Staff working with high-risk, aggressive students should take courses in nonviolent crisis prevention interventions.

Consider the Nonviolent Crisis Prevention Strategy

On a more personal note, as an elementary assistant principal within a downtown, urban setting, I utilize nonviolent crisis prevention strategies throughout the day. I effectively approach explosive children, restrain students physically, and confront irate or very upset students and parents. Crisis prevention techniques can be utilized by all staff members and will help to create a safe environment while allowing the uncontrolled student to regain control. Most often, I allow a child to cool down before I process the misbehavior with the child.

Many times the child is ready to go back to class and carry on with his or her day. Most often a child needs immediate consequences such as time-out, community service, or writing a letter of apology. Other times the child is sequestered in a private office excluded from his peers, also called in-school suspension (ISS); is sent home for a short-term suspension (therapeutic leave); or begins out-of-school suspension (OSS). I call the parent (if there is a phone) or follow up with a note home. Last, with every behavior problem, regardless of the consequence, I always document the incident for later review and substantiation for my choice of intervention.

Effectiveness of Punishment

The school administrator may need to punish a student to set an example for the rest of the student body but should not operate under the illusion that punishment will somehow remove the roots of a problem. Another serious misperception of punishment is believing the student's misbehavior will disappear forever. Campbell et al. (1990) state that there is minimal evidence that physical punishment is an effective technique for preventing misbehavior from recurring. However, it is recognized that removal of all negative consequences associated with the violation of a rule or regulation could, over time, render such rules and regulations meaningless (Gorton, 1983). Research has also found that there is the possibility that punishment may lead to other undesirable behaviors that may demonstrate more serious problems.

Students need to know that they are accountable for their behavior and that negative consequences will result from inappropriate behavior. It is realistic to impose certain punitive measures that may be necessary. However, the decision as to whether or not to punish should be based on a diagnosis of the cause of the student's behavior. When an administrator selects the type of punishment, caution should be exercised to consider the following factors:

- The cause of the misbehavior
- The severity of the offense
- The habitualness of the offender (frequency)
- The personality of the offender (how he or she responds to different punishment)

Systematically introducing punishment is controversial. Application can be tricky and accidentally trigger untoward reactions from students. Then, too, overuse of punishment can sabotage not only methodology but also respect for the teacher and the teacher's dignity. Awareness of potential problems is naturally critical. Additionally, educators may wish to follow simple guidelines when using any variation of punishment. Kameenui and Darch (1994) believe that when punishing a student, the principal or assistant principal should consider the following recommendations:

1. Use punishment sparingly.
2. Make clear to students why they are being punished.
3. Provide students with an alternative means of meeting their needs.
4. Reward students for utilizing the alternative means.
5. Avoid physical punishment if at all possible.
6. Avoid punishing while you are in a very angry or emotional state.

To be effective, punishment needs to be applied as soon after the offense as possible. Delay in administering the punishment will tend to reduce the association between the punishment and violation of the rule.

Although the pros and cons of corporal punishment have been debated for years, it is not the answer to the behavior management problems of today's urban schools. Currently, the concept of student civil rights has been used to restrict school officials' authority to control student behavior. More courts have recognized that the school must consider the rights of students in developing rules and regulations regarding discipline (Sajwaj, 1977).

In the past decades, courts have upheld students' rights to wear long hair, unorthodox clothing, and armbands, as long as these actions did not upset the rights of others to a peaceful and organized education. These issues of the 1960s and 1970s seem minor, although meaningful at the time, to the disruptions in today's classrooms. Whether dealing with discipline on the elementary or secondary level, it is important to change with the times and the changing conditions of society. Discipline is a changing phenomenon, reflecting rapidly changing mores in society. Currently, the ideal classroom management of the mass school system is expected to run independently and foster peer cooperation, traits not likely to flourish in a large urban environment.

UNDERLYING CAUSES OF DISCIPLINE PROBLEMS

When students break a rule or regulation, or when they display inappropriate behaviors, disciplinary action is required. Any disciplinary action undertaken should help the student to regain the sense of responsibility that accompanies freedom. LaVigna and Donnellan (1986) state that to accomplish this, the schools must try to do the following:

1. Understand that students can learn from mistakes made.
2. Develop a sense of cooperative effort to solve the problem rather than an attitude suggesting a struggle of students against staff and administration.
3. Help students understand and control their own behavior.
4. Deal with the underlying causes of the problems, not just the symptoms.
5. Strive to prevent the problems from occurring.

Some students simply are unable or unwilling to understand and control their behaviors. Also, the school may not always be in a position to deal with the underlying causes of a behavioral problem or to prevent the problem from occurring. For these reasons, alternative consequences are necessary to control behavior. Alternative techniques should be available to teachers and administrators as soon after the incident as possible and in keeping with the nature of the behavioral problem. In addition to dealing with the causes of a specific behavior problem, the school should try to prevent these problems from occurring. The school could provide services to help students deal with such concerns as anger control, peer relationships, and peer mediation. One resource for school-supported training is *career centers*, which supply teachers with hands-on training programs and provide valuable assistance to students in secondary schools.

Breaking a rule may not be related to underlying causes other than short-term boredom or restlessness. In some cases, corrective measures may be necessary for control purposes. However, some corrective measures are more effective than others. A few are not effective at all yet are still used in many classrooms across the nation. Almost all corrective measures currently used are *punitive in nature*. At best, these methods force the student to immediately conform to the rule or become more defiant toward the rules and authority figures trying to impose the rules (Sugai, 1995). Traditional, current corrective measures might include:

1. *The verbal reprimand.* This is the most common device and is most often used by the teacher. It may or may not be effective, even for a short period of time.

2. *The pupil–teacher conference.* This method can be an effective means of getting to the bottom of inappropriate actions. However, the conference can have overtones of punishment, depending on the approach of the teacher.

3. *After-school detention.* This popular corrective measure is not effective and does not get to the root of the problem. Many schools across the nation have abandoned detentions because it is difficult to assign staff, students do not show, and there are usually behavior problems during the assigned detention that increase the inappropriate behaviors and negative student attitudes.

4. *Community service.* This method is sometimes used when a student has defaced or destroyed school property. Usually, students can see the justice in being required to wash, sweep, or fix the areas in question. In many cases, this is not an effective consequence for elementary students, because they love to help the maintenance workers or most adults. However, if done with minimal adult contact, this method is meaningful to elementary-age children.

5. *Fines.* This monetary consequence is sometimes used in schools for such offenses as destroying property. However, principals should know that the courts have not looked with favor on fining students without an alternative punishment.

6. *Corporal punishment.* Although most states have abolished corporal punishment, it is still used in areas that have approved legal standing and have upheld the right to use corporal punishment if it is reasonable and accomplished without malice. However, the paddle or other physical means as punishment is *undesirable and ineffective, causing increased anger and defiance in most students.*

7. *Exclusion and suspension.* It is sometimes necessary to exclude a student from classes for more than one day. Suspension is a serious step to be taken only as the last resort. Most often suspension is an ineffective corrective measure because the student would rather be out of school than in school.

Traditionally, rules and regulations have spelled out specifically what students were not to do; emphasis was placed on the consequences of breaking the rules. It seems more appropriate to establish general guidelines for acceptable behavior and to work individually with students to achieve these standards. This places the matter of discipline in a positive, rather than negative, light. This action is necessary to treat students as individuals, with respect and dignity, which they may not be receiving outside the school environment. If the environment is to foster acceptable student behavior, then the school curriculum must meet the needs of each student.

ROUTINE BEHAVIOR DISTURBANCES

Educators who teach in city schools have experienced the frustration and dismay of having their class sabotaged by an aggressive, name-calling, disruptive child (Shores, Gunter et al., 1993). When a student's behavior violates the rights of others or obstructs the educational process, it is considered disruptive classroom behavior. Behaviors viewed as disruptive are a serious problem for regular classroom teachers. There is no single, precise description of disruptive behavior because children can exhibit inappropriate behaviors in a variety of ways. Students can call out, hit, make obscene noises or gestures, become verbally or physically out of control, or run through the hallways playing a catch-me game. Fagen et al. (1975), for example, have defined disruptive school behaviors as behaviors incompatible with volitional, socially acceptable efforts to master the required or assigned task; in other words, an unwanted repertoire progressively replacing a wanted, more academically based repertoire.

Educators are concerned about these behaviors not only because they disrupt the educational process but because they demand time and attention of teachers and administrators throughout each day. The teachers' feelings of stress, pressure, and emotional tension that may result affect the education process and classroom management practices. Educators and administrators want safe and productive classrooms. Although many behaviors annoy educators, there are several universal reasons why students may disrupt the classroom. Kerr and Nelson (1998) state the following reasons that students disrupt classroom activities:

- To gain your attention (positive or negative attention)
- To get the attention or approval of classmates
- To avoid doing class work
- To test the limits of your authority or to find out whether the rules will be enforced.
- To make the classroom a more interesting place

Kerr and Nelson also stated the common disruptive classroom behaviors that are documented by teachers across the nation. These include:

1. *Talking out.* Students speak without permission or interrupt the teacher or another student

2. *Out of assigned area.* Students move from their seats when not permitted, may wander around the room, and may remove items from the students' or teacher's desks.

3. *Noise.* Students create loud noises or continuous rapping/singing.

4. *Rocking.* Students lift one or more chair legs from the floor while seated in the chair, or may fall down on purpose.

5. *Noncompliance.* Students fail to initiate the appropriate responses as requested by the teacher or administrator.

6. *Physical aggression.* Students swat others or punch or engage in fistfights with other students or adults.

7. *Verbal threats.* Angry students verbally threaten other students and adults.

8. *Throwing objects.* Students throw pencils, erasers, spitballs, rubberbands, chairs, or anything within reach in the classroom.

9. *Self-abuse.* Student try to hurt themselves by biting, poking, or sticking themselves.

10. *Violating school rules.* Students clearly and blatantly violate classroom rules or engage in behavior that prevents them or others from learning (e.g., trashing materials passed out by teacher, instigating fights).

11. *Talking junk.* Students who spout specific phrases that are known to irritate certain age groups, such as saying, "Yo-Momma" or "Wanna piece of me," almost always end up in a fight with elementary- and middle-school-age students.

FACTORS INFLUENCING LACK OF SCHOOL CONTROL

To diagnose a discipline problem, the administrator and staff should investigate the validity of several alternative hypotheses for the student's misbehavior. The nature of the hypotheses will vary for different types of discipline and attendance problems. For example, Gorton (1983) states that the following school-related factors may account for a student's behavior and should be investigated:

1. The subject matter may be too difficult.

2. The subject matter may be too easy.

3. The subject matter or the class activities may not be relevant to the students' interest or needs.

4. The class assignment may be too heavy, too light, badly planned, poorly explained, or unfairly evaluated.

5. The course content or activities may not be properly sequenced for the student.

6. The seating arrangement for the student may be poor from a learning point of view.

7. There may be a personality conflict between the student and the teachers.

Each condition or any combination of these conditions may cause considerable frustration, boredom, anxiety, or hostility in a student, which could be expressed in misbehavior. However, an administrator who can ascertain the particular underlying reasons for a student's misbehavior is then in a position to know which approach to take in remedying the problem. Another consideration is the home and community environment. The school seldom has much control over a student's situation either at home or in the neighborhood. However, both factors may be important in causing a disruption in the classroom.

While there are situations where the school should look at the home or the community for causes of a student's misbehavior, frequently the source of problems is found within the school. However, knowing where the problem is and *doing something about it* are two distinct issues. Correcting the source of problems may be obstructed by politically or rigidly defined school disciplinary policies. According to Walker et al. (1995), most schools fail to respond to discipline effectively due to rigid interpretation or a breakdown of the general criteria for evaluating student discipline policies. Gorton (1983) discusses the following school discipline policies and procedures:

1. The school's discipline policies and procedures should be based on established school board policies.

2. There should be overall agreement among students, teachers, parents, and administrators about the philosophy and objectives of the disciplinary policies and procedures of the school.

3. The school should maintain only disciplinary policies and procedures that have an educational purpose, are administratively feasible, and are legally enforceable.

4. Policies and procedures on student behavior should be stated in positive forms as much as possible, and student responsibility rather than misbehavior should be stressed.

5. The policies and procedures governing student behavior should be written in clear, understandable language and be presented in student, teacher, and parent handbooks that are reviewed at the beginning of each school year.

6. The consequences of violating a rule or regulation should be made explicit and commensurate with the nature of the violation.

7. The rationale supporting the rules, procedures, and consequences governing student behavior should be clearly communicated to students and should be enforced fairly and consistently.

Failure of Teachers and Administrators to Respond Effectively

Many teachers begin teaching without knowing how to speed up or slow down behaviors. Some teachers do not provide accelerating consequences (e.g., reinforcers) at all. These teachers rely on the assumption that children are supposed to be good or should learn for the sake of learning, without receiving any reinforcers for their behaviors. Some teachers do not provide immediate consequences; other teachers do not provide effective consequences. A consequence may not be effective for several reasons; just because a consequence works as a reinforcer for one child does not necessarily mean that it will work for another child (Shores, Gunter et al., 1993).

A consequence may also lose its effectiveness if it is overused. If a teacher frequently uses the same reinforcer, it then becomes less effective. The following definitions provide a consistent frame of discussion within the next few chapters:

Consequences

A consequence is a reward (reinforcer) or punishment (punisher) after a response or action. A consequence may be too small or not large enough. Quantity depends on the child and behavior in question. For some children, physical proximity or a light touch is effective. For others, a behavior contract or desk chart that is rated every 30 minutes using stars or checks for immediate feedback is suitable. It is much more effective to present sequential consequences to a child than a single large consequence.

Another important consideration regarding consequences is that learning becomes automatic and noncontingent on consequences once rewards or punishers are effectively and systematically used. This idea counters the intuitive myth that using consequences makes students overreliant on "bribes" or "getting secondary gains" for good behavior, that appropriate behavior should come from moral inertia instead of from external incentives. Contrariwise, methodically used rewards and punishers that are later faded out as part of the learning process produce better-trained students who retain their skills without wanting or receiving rewards and punishers (i.e., rule-governed behaviors).

Praise

When praise is used as a reinforcer, it may not be effective unless it is directed at a specific behavior.

Corrective Feedback

Alerting students to their errors in a positive manner, immediately after they respond, may facilitate the correct response. Corrective feedback must also specify the *topography and function* of the preferred response. Topography refers to *what the preferred behavior is.* Function refers to *what value or consequences it produces.* For example, asking children to remain seated when they are up socializing with other students requires (1) telling then to sit down and return to task and (2) telling them the reward (or punisher) for appropriate sitting.

Sustained Feedback

This involves staying with students who gave an incorrect response and leading them to the correct one with cues and possible examples of the correct answer.

Content-Specific Feedback

This involves offering specific feedback, regardless if the answer was correct or incorrect, for example, when teachers say, "I like the way you raised your hand," or "Thank-you for responding today," or "The answer you gave was very creative."

Positive Discipline

This is an approach that is effective in teaching children self-discipline, responsibility, cooperation, and problem-solving skills.

Some teachers and administrators do not consistently present a consequence immediately following a behavior every time the behavior occurs. Also, some teachers present too many consequences when they are trying to alter behaviors. Once a behavior is learned, it is more likely to be maintained if it is only occasionally followed by rewards or consequences. Educators must remember, in teaching new behaviors, to reduce learning into measurable and achievable steps. Learning begins where the student's behavior currently is and moves toward where you want the child's behavior to progress.

Most educators are aware that the school curriculum must have relevance and meaning to real-life experiences. Although it is difficult to develop and implement more humanistic and current programming, there is now a broad base of support for school programs that extend learning beyond cognitive skills and knowledge. An imaginative educational program, as the following chapters demonstrate, concentrates on areas such as self-control, motivation, diversity, peer mediation, and other alternative methods.

Effective programming must integrate emotional, cognitive, and interpersonal learning components. If these areas can be established within the framework of a systematized, connected curriculum, then real potential for a powerful impact on both the student and the teaching environment exists. Throughout this book, the practical incorporation of these techniques within the public school setting is also be discussed.

RATIONALE AND PURPOSES OF TEACHING SELF-CONTROL

Gold and Mann (1982) suggest that the most direct and enduring means of altering behavior and overcoming disturbances that are associated with discipline problems is the combination of nontraditional and traditional approaches. A specialized curriculum based on the needs of the population or needs of an individual must be available and practical. Alternative approaches to instruction must be presented within a context of positive relationship and sensitive teaching. Alternative approaches offer an effective, consistent means of minimizing disruptions and inappropriate behaviors in the classroom.

Children who are behaviorally disruptive are likely to experience many other social and emotional difficulties as well. This is due to the fact that the child's inappropriate behaviors trigger negative responses from others. The negative responses then contribute to the child's feelings of inadequacy, badness, deficiency, and social rejection. Although different roots for impulsive behaviors exist, our basic belief is that major problems for impulsive children derive from learned behaviors rather than from innate causes. Therefore, the authors maintain that impulsive behavior creates profound difficulties for social and emotional adjustment and self-control. The emphasis is then on building adaptive controls, interrupting self-defeating behavior cycles, and altering and possibly preventing serious behavior and learning problems.

Given the various ramifications of disruptive behaviors, there are several purposes for having instructional methods and procedures aimed at altering self-control of school-age children. According to Allen et al. (1983), the purposes are as follows:

1. To reduce disruptiveness in the classroom, enhancing an environment conducive to learning.

2. To prevent behavior and learning disorders.

3. To strengthen the emotional and cognitive capacities that children need in order to cope with school requirements.

4. To build control and coping skills that allow for an effective and socially acceptable choice of action.

5. To enhance value to the teacher–learner and educational process.

6. To promote a more desirable educational balance between cognitive and affective development than that which currently exists.

7. To act on the commitment that all children can learn and become productive citizens.

CHARACTERISTICS OF SCHOOLS WITH GOOD DISCIPLINE

The Phi Delta Kappa Commission on Discipline (1982) conducted a study to identify schools with good discipline and determine what characteristics they exhibited. It also described the activities they use to achieve good discipline. Schools with exemplary discipline exhibited the following characteristics:

1. These schools foster good discipline by creating a total school environment that is conducive to good discipline rather than adopting isolated practices to deal with discipline problems.

2. Most of the educators view their school as a place where staff and students come to work and to experience the success of doing something well.

3. These schools are student-oriented.

4. These schools focus on causes of discipline rather than symptoms.

5. Programs in these schools emphasize positive behavior and use preventive measures rather than traditional actions to improve discipline.

6. These schools adopt alternative or nontraditional practices to meet their own identified needs and to reflect their own styles of operation.

7. The school administrators play a key role in making these schools what they are and in how they deal with disruptive students.

8. The programs in these schools often result from the teamwork of a capable principal and assistant principal or some other staff member who has the personal leadership qualities that complement those of the principal.

9. The staff of these schools believe in their school and in what its students can do. The staff also expend unusual amounts of energy to make that belief come true.

10. Teachers in these schools handle all or most of the routine discipline problems.

11. The majority of these schools develop stronger than average ties with parents and with community agencies.

12. These schools are open to critical review and evaluation from a wide variety of school and community sources.

Effectively administered schools provide consistent standards for classroom management. While teachers may vary in their disciplinary philosophies, uniformly adapted procedures for all classrooms bridge this difference in philosophy and allow administrators to monitor and troubleshoot problems that arise. Schools using uniform disciplinary guidelines specifically tailored for classroom disruption yield the following general results:

1. Total management packages appear more effective than separate components or combinations of components (Walker et al., 1976; Walker & Hops, 1993).

2. The most important component of management systems is the application of contingent extrinsic and intrinsic consequences (Hayes, 1976; Porterfield et al., 1976).

3. The optimum management package, particularly for highly disruptive students, appears to be a combination of group and individual contingencies (Polsgrove & Nelson, 1982; Walker, 1995).

SUMMARY

Planning and operating a positive and productive classroom environment are important elements of success in teaching students with minor to serious behavior problems. Without effective behavior management, teachers and students do not have a safe and productive learning environment. This chapter provides information about disruptive behaviors in the classroom, identifies the urban school-age child, and discusses failures of educators to effectively respond to the needs of our urban children. The widespread occurrence of inappropriate behaviors in the schools represents a serious challenge for current educators. For the urban child, disruptive behavior may reflect a breakdown of personal resources for coping with school expectations and the impulsive actions of negative, maladaptive reactions to a stressful living environment.

The challenge is evident. Students must come to believe themselves capable of controlling their own behavior, even in the face of frustration and despair outside the school. All children must discover that through self-directed efforts and alternative methods, they can effectively cope with difficulty rather than be victimized by exposure to overwhelming demands.

Johns and Carr (1995) state that the process of learning needs to become a sequence of challenges and responses through which our urban school-age children find satisfaction. Intrinsic reward derives from the progressive development of technology, life skills and community-based training and preparing for positive social interactions in the adult world. These resources allow children to make an effective and responsible choice of action in their daily lives.

There is little doubt that school discipline problems are becoming more serious in frequency, duration, and intensity, especially in our metropolitan societies across America. Uncorrected school discipline can be detrimental to a safe and orderly school environment. Revising traditional standards and adopting new policies are not easy, but exigencies for this effort are stronger than ever. Policy changes must include expanding beliefs about discipline, behavior management, positive discipline, and practical as well as meaningful curriculum, introducing nontraditional instructional methods, programs, and assessments. Most importantly, educators must be open to change. Teaching and policy-making habits are hard to break; but as disordered urban students increase in numbers, teachers may find change a necessity for survival.

Why Traditional Behavior Modification Fails with Urban Children

Douglas H. Ruben

Teen violence and aggressive behavior are akin to nuclear destruction. Once an adversarial nation secretly manufactures uranium into nuclear explosives, it threatens bordering nations and triggers worldwide alert to this crisis. Violence in youth also begins in benign ways. Silently evolving from infancy to early adolescence are emotional deprivations and forms of punishment shaping an adversarial child. The grown adolescent rebels innocuously until his or her actions trumpet alert in adult observers. Defiance is no longer a "passing stage" but becomes a real and disturbing threat to the community. Parents, teachers, principals, and clergy all collectively conspire to squelch this adolescent deviance before it progresses out of control and is, in a word, a *crisis*.

Not only does adolescent delinquency escalating out of control threaten the community, but innocent victims afflicted by its destructive effects are never the same. Devastated victims of Andrew Wurst's shooting spree at Parker Middle School in Edinboro, Pennsylvania, watched in horror as their bloodied peers dropped on the dance floor. The nightmare of Wurst's shooting left indelible and painful images in eighth graders' minds. So, too, the Westside Middle School shooting in Jonesboro, Arkansas, left four girls and one teacher fatally wounded at the hands of two teenage boys. Teen shooting crimes also ravaged the cities of Pearl, Mississippi, and five months later in Bethel, Alaska. Deviant youngsters who turned aggressively violent murdered their peers and unleashed tyranny on rural and urban communities. By the time violence hit Littleton, Colorado, panic of copycat shootings circulating high schools put the American culture on notice.

Sadly, this chapter is not going to stop the murderers. Rising juvenile crime marks a tragic pivot in urban communities. Underage students resorting to violence and using terroristic tactics represent a new wave of problems in depressed urban schools. Frustrated teachers and administrators shocked by the torrent of crime respond swiftly with zero-tolerance policies, smaller classes, and increased community police. They recently even began suspending students who merely talk about violence but are not physically aggressive. Violent acts also sparked a Springfield, Illinois, company to offer teachers insurance policies against assault. Politically, state and federal programs are cracking down on potentially dangerous students and using their full arsenal to create safer schools. The ambitious initiatives include (1) positive and expectations and clear rules for students, (2) positive identification of students and staff, (3) parent awareness of safely storing and securing all guns, (4) creation of a safe-haven approach where parents pledge their children will visit nongun and nondrug homes, and (5) student access to support groups to cope with life stressors.

Safer-school campaigns are laudable. But the downside of them is this: counter-deviant behavioral methods currently applied in schools may be too general. They are too nebulous and optimistic to combat the rising sophistication of aggressors and their crimes.

This chapter responds to the increasing specialization of behavioral methodology necessary for high-risk, inner-city students. It distinctly reviews inherent flaws in common school behavioral interventions and revises these strategies for crime abatement. Behavioral interventions for *regular* classroom deviance already are prolific (Bergan & Caldwell, 1995; Carpenter & McKee-Higgins, 1996; Kazdin, 1975; Sulzer-Azaroff & Mayer, 1972; O'Leary & O'Leary, 1976), and widely acceptable among school personnel. The literature is replete with exemplary, stepwise interventions for accelerating academic performance and decelerating disruptive classroom misbehavior.

Methods employing behavior modification for *high-risk* or *juvenile* children, however, are less extensive and largely derivative from adult interventions (e.g., Burchard & Harig, 1976; Burchard & Lane, 1982; Nietzel, 1979; Van Hasselt & Hersen, 1998). Operant procedures range from token economies to differential reinforcement and draw support from research studies that strongly generalize results to ethnically, racially, and culturally diverse populations (Grossman, 1990; Rutherford & Nelson, 1995). Universality of methods among diverse groups inherently implies that procedures used for rural, affluent urban students should be equally as effective with urban, multicultural students.

Unfortunately, this assumption fails miserably when realizing there is a multiplicity of intercultural variables untested empirically. Variables endemic to urban street behavior may be strangely impervious to traditional behavioral methods. Such variables may include (1) normalcy of crime, (2) cultural reinforcement of aggression, (3) social reinforcement for self-protection, and (4) punishment for civil obedience and respecting authorities (cf. Locke, 1997; Markus & Kitayama, 1998). The dearth of experimental research supporting the validity and efficacy of behavioral methods with these variables thus accounts for the current chapter.

Examined are pitfalls of school behavioral programs and parameters of effective behavioral interventions with inner-city urban students. While duplicating, to some extent, reviews of methodology expected in subsequent chapters, analyses here are more technically specific on *why procedures fail behaviorally and how to correct the contingencies, no matter what procedure is used.* The first section on pitfalls covers contingency defects, vicarious interference by teachers, cultural irrelevance of contingencies, and nongenerality of training goals. Optimistic resolutions to these problems appear in the second section. Discussion covers procedures for generalizable behavioral urban programs, programmed sensitivity training, and goal-directed training.

PITFALLS OF SCHOOL BEHAVIORAL PROGRAMS

Acceptable protocols for behavioral methods require two fundamental conditions: reliability and consistency. *Reliability* suggests implementing procedures directly as written or agreed upon by the behavioral engineers (i.e., teachers, case managers, facilitators, peer mediators). Reliability also involves *two or more* independent applicators of the behavioral intervention, following the same procedure, that produce identical or fairly equivalent results in the students' behavior. *Consistency* addresses the accurate duplication of procedures each and every time the procedure occurs. Accuracy applies not only to many uses of a procedure with *one* student but also to a multitude of procedural applications for *many* students.

In a perfect world, reliability and consistency also are pristine; they exist among all users of behavioral procedures. As methods become fallible, reliability and consistency gradually decay, and this decreases uniformity of interventions among users. The problem arises, naturally, that in school settings where procedural imperfection rapidly deteriorates to chaos and randomness, control over aggressive, violent student behavior is nonexistent. Failure to exert behavior change is not always due to bad procedures; nor is it genuinely the fault of uncaring or retaliatory teachers and administrators. The fault lies clearly in another domain. Skinner (1972) put it eloquently this way:

All these measures fail because they do not give the student adequate reasons for studying and learning. Punishment gave him a reason ... but if we are to avoid unwanted byproducts we must find nonpunitive forms. It is not an impossible assignment. The "reasons" why men behave are to be found among the consequences of their behavior—what, to put it roughly, they "get out of behaving in given ways." ... The contingencies, rather than the reinforcers, are the important things. (p. 227)

Contingencies, Not Consequences

Contingency defects plague the most ideal programs. A basic contingency describes the relationship between actual or observable student behaviors and outcomes produced by those behaviors. Engineered outcomes, as when teaching students reading skills, are precise and predictable. Clearly defined instructions prompting reading skills bring about expected changes; even sluggish readers, for example, are covered by the contingencies. They begin remedial steps to repetitively improve word pronunciation, recognition, and comprehension. Their reading deficiencies or other related problems (e.g., attentional deficits) do not derail the instructional sequence; reading programs build in a contingency for slow readers. A logarithm of learning steps first strengthens reading prerequisites and then alleviates bad habits impeding mispronunciation. By isolating reading stumbling blocks, students predictably progress through a series of remedial, task-analytic steps that correct reading mistakes until they can master the lesson.

Contingencies used in school for basic skills (reading, writing, arithmetic, etc.) thus have been efficient for regular and special education students. But when fundamental skills such as reading and writing get delayed by problems unrelated to reading, writing, and arithmetic such as, for example, violent outbursts, instructional contingencies to "get back on track" are ineffective. Violent outbursts, chronic verbal provocation, and peer fighting are obviously *topographically and functionally* different from word mispronunciation or mathematical miscalculations and require different contingencies (cf. Delprato, 1986; Ruben, 1990).

Topographically different refers to the form, shape, and other properties defining the response. Aggressively uncontrollable behaviors, for example, are intense and frequent, may last long (high duration), and consist of many concurrent or sequential patterns; concurrent patterns are the simultaneous responses acting in tandem such as students yelling and throwing chairs, verbally threatening and grabbing a student, exposing a weapon and aiming it. Sequential patterns pertain to an orderly ritual or routine through which responses repeatedly occur: a provoking student may verbally escalate and then run out of the classroom; a self-mutilator may pick at his skin for several minutes before pricking it with pins and cutting it with scissors.

Functionally different means there are visible outcomes observed among teachers, students, and administrators affected by the offensive students' concurrent and sequential responses. These changes are likely to recur both *before and after* future occurrences of the concurrent and sequential responses. An emotionally impaired student, for example, who impulsively slaps another student produces several discernible side effects. First, the victim may verbally or physically retaliate, inciting other classmates to vigilantism; bystanders either may applaud or repudiate the victimizer, further propagating his actions. Second, aggressive teachers may verbally escalate and repeat reprimands; passive teachers may submissively overlook the infraction and ignore the perpetrator; level-headed teachers may quickly squelch discordance and mediate rising tensions among feuding students. Beside teachers, the transgression leaves an indelible emotional imprint on student observers. One offense or many repeated offenses generate fear and anticipation over anxiously expecting another assaultive outburst from the delinquent student.

Victims, bystanders, and teacher all experience the immediate and residual effects of an impulsive student's striking another student. *Functionally, violent behaviors produce specific and broad consequences for everybody involved; nobody is excluded* (Kazdin, 1985; Ruben, 1986). Exposed students react with fear, hostility, and vengeance, all of which clearly interfere with the class curriculum and become incompatible to academic learning. The assaulted victims distrust the teacher, distrust the offensive student, and are hypersensitive to recurrent classroom outbursts. *In other words, victims and bystanders are as much a target for intervention as is the assailant.* Contingencies focusing on multiple students, including victimizer, victim, and bystanders, stand a far better chance of defusing potentially explosive classroom disruptions and restoring attention to the learning objectives than contingencies that singularly focus on the victimizer.

Thinking in "multiple contingencies" challenges the myth that correction of only bad students ensures classroom control. Restoring control goes beyond individualized behavioral interventions. The goal of intervention is not only to stop bad behavior but to redesign classroom contingencies aimed at *risk reduction, to reduce acuity of problems emanating from any student involved in classroom disturbance*. Aggressive students, for example, sent to the principal's office may temporarily eliminate classroom disruption and superficially appear to restore tranquillity for teacher and other students; even permanent removal of this bad seed from class provides only an ephemeral solution. Eliminating the student and problem behavior, however, are smoke screens to the most significant problem: *the other students*. Risk reduction entails both isolating the aggressor's violent responses *and* establishing concurrent contingencies for other students to feel safe and productive in the classroom.

A procedure for the violent assailant such as token economy, for example, may attenuate his or her rude remarks and out-of-seat, off-task behaviors; but neighboring students previously traumatized by the assailant's behavior may remain hypervigilant and distrustful and feel trepidation, waiting for the assailant to strike again. Their anticipatory arousal arises from feeling unprotected and *inescapably and unavoidably exposed to potential confrontation*. A token economy implemented for the assailant *and* neighboring students, however, both relieves the neighboring students' anxiety and defuses their propensity to overreact if the assailant's violence reemerges.

The exigency for multiple contingencies in producing systemic classroom change is unfortunately rare in actual practice. Special educators exclusively target behavioral interventions for students at risk and not for emotionally impacted students not at risk (Johnson & Pugach, 1996; Rutherford & Nelson, 1995). Griffin (1998), for example, interviewed 60 exceptional education classroom teachers on procedures they regularly use to ameliorate classroom misbehavior. The majority reported using more than one procedure and abundantly depended on time-out and reprimands. Worse yet, some teachers kept delinquent students in time-out all day—up to six hours—while, presumably, in the view of other classmates. One can only imagine the elevated anxiety classmates felt while observing a volatile aggressor confined for six hours but not *changed behaviorally*. Just as a caged animal turns savage when released, so an unchanged aggressor lethally explodes when time-out expires. Prolonged confinement predictably exacerbates aggressive behavior to the point of uncontrollability and, consequently, to the detriment of other classmates.

Failure of teachers to specify contingencies dually controlling troublemaker and nontroublemaker is an egregious mistake in behavioral management. Changes that positively or negatively occur in one student *always cause corresponding changes in all other students within the setting* (Fox & Conroy, 1995). As acting-out students worsen, risk of nondisruptive students' becoming agitated and reactionary increases in probability. Likewise, troublemakers whose behaviors progressively and reliably improve ease classroom tensions and proportionally decrease malcontent among the observant classmates. Thus, methods that distinctly and simultaneously employ contingencies for both good and bad students address the covariance effects of urban classrooms.

Vicarious Interference

Preschool and adolescent aggressive students who disrupt classrooms are usually the central target of school intervention. Teachers hurriedly implement strategies, and principals and counselors urgently respond by contacting the students' parents or supporting staff during the intervention. Administrators and instructors collaboratively assemble a troubleshooting system theoretically capable of defusing explosive students, reassuring safety and security for teachers and restoring a semblance of peace in the classroom. When this system works, and all parties competently fulfill their roles, regulatory control over student misbehavior permits normal instruction to occur. When the system fails, mistakes cause disregulation of aggressive behavior, and classrooms and teacher remain in jeopardy. Urban schools face the latter predicament more frequently and may inadvertently blame the ubiquity of student disobedience for behavioral program failures.

A closer inspection of teacher–student variables may shed different light on program failures. While student delinquency is prolific, reasons for teachers' and administrators' defecting from consistent and reliable programs may be due to a variable called *vicarious interference*. In vicarious interference severely behavior-disordered students cause teachers to personalize and internalize perceived aversive qualities of the students' behavior. Affected teachers who suffer stress, hostility, and helplessness feel powerless over controlling problem classrooms; they may develop avoidance and escape patterns wherein they counter the aversive properties of their students either by acting aggressively, ignoring the student, or aborting the problem. Some instructors even quit teaching or ask to be reassigned from special education to regular education classrooms (Billingsley & Cross, 1991; Lawrenson & McKinnon, 1982). Avoidance and escape behaviors arise progressively out of ineffectiveness of personal resources to avert the *arbitrary, random or unpredictable onset of aversive stimulation* (Ruben, 1993a; Weinner, 1969).

Gunter et al. (1994) empirically explored this phenomenon. They argued that teachers naturally respond to aversive behavior by avoidance and escape-motivated behaviors, typically causing a vicious reciprocal and coercive interaction. The *reciprocal* interaction consists of mutually exchanged discord between student and teacher as aversiveness intensifies. The *coercive* interaction occurs when both teacher and student resort almost compulsively to countercontrols, that is, act negatively toward each other out of desperation to delay or avert contact with aversive actions. In this respect, the reciprocal/exchange theory of Patterson and Reid (1970) is applicable to teacher–student conflict in classrooms (Shores, Jack et al., 1993).

Avoidance or escape directly derives from the teachers' rising frustrations at insurmountable and repetitive encounters with punitive students. Teachers feel the locus of control is external, not internal, and personally solving the student crisis is impossible. Verbal reprimands are useless, administrator support is weak, and aggressors appear immune to tokens, peer mediation, or simplified reinforcement methods. A disillusioned teacher vicariously reacts to daily classroom conflict with avoidance and escape, producing decremental effects on instructor and instruction. Teacher attrition rates and burnout clearly rank as primordial side effects (Fimian, 1983; Greer & Greer, 1992). The teacher's personal stress also contributes to serious mismanagement of behavioral interventions that may reverse student progress or excacerbate student aggression. Reviewed here are four particular interferences on methodology and their untoward effects on behavior: These include *procedural decay, contingency bias, hidden agenda,* and *nonreciprocal outcomes.*

Procedural Decay

Procedural decay is the inadvertent and gradual deterioration of administering contingencies accurately. Decay arises after strategies using simple or complex methods have been in place for extended periods and go unchecked. Variability occurs in the delivery of consequences or in defining target behaviors meriting reinforcers or punishers. Criteria fluctuate and unintentionally overlap with target behaviors for other strategies, and eventually consistency of application is lost. This mistake produces two types of decay. The first is *decay across different teachers.* Here the precision of methods equally attenuates among many teachers concurrently working with one student; each teacher implements a slightly or profoundly different procedure for the target behavior. Although on paper, written contingencies specify the procedural steps and operationally qualify the behavior, in practice the procedure drifts from the written methods and behavior definitions. Behavior modifiers respond instinctively after a while with vague memories of the exact methodology.

A second decay is *across many behaviors of one student.* One teacher inundated with several behavioral management plans for one student may not have a photographic memory. Explicit recall of detailed procedures is diffiicult for similar or even dissimilar target behaviors, and, invariably, strategies may intermingle or be reversed. Intermingling procedures occur when several steps from one behavior management plan inadvertently combine with steps from another set of contingencies, forming a brand-new set of undefined procedures doomed for failure. Reversed procedures are even worse. Entire methods, instead of only one or two steps from one behavior management plan, switch with steps from another behavior management plan, risking both chaos and untoward effects on target behaviors. Imagine, for example, reversing token economy for on-task, sitting behaviors with overcorrection for peer-hitting behaviors. Off-task students might be instructed to publicly apologize to the class and write an elaborate paper debasing classroom disturbances. In the reversal, peer-hitting students lose tokens and delayed opportunities for reward exchange.

So, why is this a problem? First, public apologies or written essays on classroom disturbance *provide immediate opportunity for off-task behaviors and thereby reinforce competing or inappropriate behaviors.* Negatively reinforced behaviors (i.e., reinforced for "getting out of something"—on-task behavior) would dangerously increase, not decrease off-task, disruptive behaviors and subsequently exacerbate an uncontrollable classroom. Second, removal or nonexchanges of tokens for peer-hitting behaviors are about as useless as using an umbrella with holes during a thunderstorm. Tokens as reinforcers shape behavior only if there are no other accessible consequences powerfully competing with tokens that sustain peer-hitting behaviors. In this case, *hitting produces social reinforcers more powerful than earning or losing tokens.* Aggressive students thereby remain immune to token economy, whereas the correct consequence—*public apology and written essay*—might decrease the target behavior by humiliating the student with loss of social reinforcers (i.e., peers see the student as vulnerable, weak, and undeserving of a reputation).

Contingency Bias

Contingency bias is not particularly found in behavioral literature on methodology except for discussion surrounding therapist insensitivity during initial assessment phases (Hersen, 1976). "Bias" means subjective intolerance to one or many factors written into the behavioral management program that negatively influence the implementer and cause inaccurate application. Personal bias covers a wide spectrum of variables ranging from the target behavior to selected consequences. Target behaviors that pose moral or ethical objection or that seem recidivistically destructive in the teacher's classroom may be perceived with animosity beyond what is necessary for change methodology. Likewise, consequences regarded as lenient, ineffective, or "babying the student" receive little respect and serious effort in being properly delivered during a behavioral plan.

In the worst scenario, contingency bias can be propelled by blatant disbelief in behavior modification and sabotage of schoolwide behavior plans that disastrously potentiate misbehavior. Examples abound of failed programs derailed early on by self-righteous, uncooperative educators who take matters into their own hands. *School vigilantes* assertively decry the demoralization of student behaviors and unilaterally believe harsher interventions are mandatory versus least restrictive or reinforcing options (Elliott, 1993; Huesmann et al., 1996). Barring juvenile gang members from lunch cafeterias or police arrest for graffiti of gang signs on school buildings all employ harsh penalties. Pro-arrest policies to aggressively stop perpetrators of school offenses thus seem a natural next step; already many communities sponsor police monitoring and strict action against aggravated battery against women (cf. Bourg & Stock, 1994).

As swift and decisive social policies enforce offender-control steps, educators are likely to adopt this mentality in dismissing behavioral plans as ineffective. In-school plans that deviate from cultural mandates automatically may be rejected on principle. However, educators are not zealots. Outrightly refusing to use a behavior plan may appear insubordinate. Alternatively, they diplomatically and genuinely concede to behavior-change contingencies for students, knowing internally the interventions diametrically oppose their values. This discrepancy leads to carelessness, discontinuity of steps, resistance of progressive ideas, and denial of any student improvement attributable to the behavior plan.

The major drawback of contingency bias is a syllogism that concludes that delinquent students *never can change*. It goes like this: *if bad students really reformed, they would have to serve jail time or suffer restitutional penalties for their crimes. Since they do not serve jail time or suffer any restitutional penalty (but rather, get reinforcers and polite treatment), they cannot reform*. Simple-minded as this circular reasoning may appear, many educators regard it as conventional wisdom. Values of society contrasting with values implied in a behavioral plan thus may seem innocuous but are serious detriments to a successful intervention.

Hidden Agenda

Hidden agendas are savage obstructions to effective programs. Teachers or administrators may ideally follow contingencies according to Hoyle until they let their own biases or *similar experiences prejudice objective intervention*. When this occurs, two types of interferences occur. First is when behavior modifiers positively identify with reinforcing programs similar to what they received years ago as students or in adulthood. For example, teachers who accelerated their math skills or reduced misbehavior in elementary school when placed on a token economy may readily share their own student's enthusiasm. Students may feel the teacher's excitement and show enormous inertia to work through the system. Then, too, overenthusiastic token economy users may overlook obvious pitfalls in its application. Lower scores, increased tardiness, and attrition all may slip past the teacher as weak token systems decay or collapse.

In a second interference, teachers negatively identify with the program or behavior. Outwardly supportive users of behavioral methods may be "closet heretics." Their history or "reactional biography" (Delprato, 1980) may consist of many episodes as child, student, parent, or teacher attempting behavioral interventions and discovering to their disdain that methods failed. Cumulatively, these unpleasant memories contaminate the behavior modifier's unmotivated use of procedures and expectation of futility. Unintentionally but inevitably, skepticism undermines the teacher's capacity to effectively troubleshoot program failures. Rather, crippled programs quickly are declared "dead" without postmortem autopsy to evaluate flaws in the program and improve upon mistakes for subsequent applications.

Nonreciprocal Outcomes

Administrators who enforce implementation of behavioral programs make a grand assumption. They assume execution of the program follows a linear sequence of *teacher to student, where the student is a passive recipient of instructions*. In behavior contracting, for example, components of the agreement may include student *and* teacher input regarding the target behaviors and consequences earned for meeting criteria. Consensual contracts purport reciprocal and joint decisions but actually are not reciprocal. Student input rarely covers *the choice and topography of target behavior*. Even selection of reinforcing or punishing consequences is predetermined; it derives from an existing pool of options already established by the teacher or administrator. Available rewards to choose from may or may not appeal to students or not consist of *functional reinforcers practical in students' daily lives.*

Nonreciprocal methodology, then, is when contingency behavioral management imposes a standard of performance or selection of consequences onto students without preassessing the feasibility of the contingencies. Hypothetically, the contingencies may be perfect; however, for uninvolved students, contingencies may appear meaningless and unrealistic since students cannot identify with the contingencies.

Peer mediation protocols, for instance, call for well-behaved, student arbitrators to act as judges, jurors, and therapists. They are referees who render action as fair or unfair and negotiate settlements with belligerent students to avert teacher–student confrontations. Theoretically, using students who can relate to other students is a sound system. Unfortunately, students who teachers believe are fine mediators and even popular in school may be lack credibility among many students, especially those in gangs. Members of the Vice Lords may object to peer mediators in rival gangs such as the Folk People. Likewise, mediators who may commit territorial violations; they may trespass onto one gang's turf and inadvertently spark violence instead of peacemaking. Gang membership in inner-city schools is so pervasive that teachers must *communicate with diverse samples of students to determine peer-mediator candidates acceptable to gangs and nongangs* (cf. Hall & Whitaker, 1998).

Cultural Irrelevance of Contingencies

Defective contingencies result from a myriad of inherent structural problems in the intervention. Already seen is that artifact bias such as subjective teacher history can negatively influence or even sabotage programs. Sabotage in methodology may also arise from inconsistent, unreliable, or poorly constructed procedures penetrable by student and teacher apathy. Still a third problem plaguing behavioral methods is the *cultural irrelevance of contingencies.* "Relevance" refers to rewards, punishers, or behaviors occasioned by these consequences that are socially meaningful to students. In basic research, questions about socially meaningful variables refer to *external validity.* Likewise, in school settings, externally valid contingencies consist of instructional prompts (i.e., antecedents), states of learning (i.e., establishing operation; Michael, 1982), and outcomes (reinforcers, punishers).

A student residing in the city "projects," for example, may function with an entirely different set of contingencies from that of affluent students transported from outlying neighborhoods. Differences produced from widely heterogeneous groups of urban students can unknowingly destroy behavioral interventions from the outset, despite the program's efficacy in rural or homogeneously based urban schools. Four unsuspecting cultural variables may interfere with social validity of procedures. These include *noncontingent reward systems; contingencies perceived as conformity; rewards considered bribery and barter; and punishment perceived as learning.*

Noncontingent Reward Systems

Underprivileged students whose parents live below the poverty line may experience a different world from that of students from professional or dual-income families. Austere budgets call for radical means of survival against hunger, sickness, homelessness, and family desertion. Students acclimated to social dilapidation learn the rule that rewards are comparatively few and accessible only to aggressive seekers, not passive bystanders. Premium rewards such as food, clothing, shelter, and illicit drugs are salvaged, not earned, and require impulsive action before somebody else discovers the limited resources. Seizure of goods in a low-supply, inner-city "economy" thus produces an "inner-city" contingency fostering rules and behaviors. The rule is simple: *rewards do not have to be earned. They are first come, first served.*

Students operating on these contingencies may be resistant to behavior methods inherently involving the conditional *if, then* of "If a behavior occurs, then (reinforcing or punishing) consequences are forthcoming." Implied associations between target behaviors and entitlement of rewards deviate from the inner-city-minded-student, who may not perceive any connection between *good behaviors and good outcomes.* Rather, good behaviors such as cooperation and self-sacrifice contradict the governing rules of cultural survival. These rules implicitly state that good behaviors lose opportunities for rewards, whereas aggressively forceful behaviors gain the rewards.

For example, in an elementary class where two students receive an equal number of math problems to solve before recess, one child may finish efficiently and enjoy recess; recess functions as an establishing operation or motivator for task completion. The other student neither finishes the math problems nor cares if math problems are completed prior to, or after, recess. Failure to complete the math may not be a learning disorder (i.e., not knowing how to perform the equations), but rather a *contingency disorder.* Incongruence between behaviors and rewards impedes the student from trying to earn or deserve anything since all rewards are perceived as fair game for whoever is quicker and smarter.

Contingencies Perceived as Conformity

Another problem is that contingencies explicitly stated in behavioral methods have a negative connotation. Operational definitions of behavior and consequences automatically signal misperceptions of coercion. Urban teens surrounded by gangs and neighborhood crime may live in unsupervised households with single parents working odd shifts. As they are left unattended, with nebulous ideas about self-sufficiency and inconsistent lifestyle routines, rarely do household or personal rules dictate social behaviors. Frequently, choices to eat, sleep, or recreate with peers are arbitrary or largely dependent on noncontingent relationships between what the student does and what others do. For example, friends may hang out at the "crib" (house) waiting for their buddies, without clearly knowing the time schedule for their friends' arrival. Randomly waiting at home neither increases nor decreases the probability of their friends' forthcoming visit.

Undefined contingencies evoke arbitrary or *superstitious behaviors* (Zeiler, 1972). Superstitious behaviors consist of noncausal, spontaneous occurrences of behavior without any regard to ongoing situations. The reason the same behavior recurs is that extraneous reinforcers, unrelated to the behavior, unintentionally and unpredictably arise. These oddball reinforcers emerging out of nowhere shape the behavior and teach a person to reasonably expect similar reinforcers in the future. For example, adolescents left alone may have irregular eating habits but always "know" they will eat *something* by nighttime. As evening approaches, borrowed money or raiding a friend's kitchen provides a meal. However, none of the adolescent's behaviors five hours earlier predicted meals that evening. Meals, in other words, depended on the random correlation between food-seeking behaviors and actual meals obtained.

By contrast, predictably defined contingencies represent such a colossal change for the adolescent urban student that they simply lack a way to effectively respond. Clearly stated behaviors and consequences *force the student to act routinely and in an orderly way,* two elements not in their repertoire. The only other place they possibly received routine and orderly contingencies (e.g., if, thens) was in church. Sermons and the code of conduct demanded of sitting in church constituted a coercive, not a self-selecting, process. Consequently, a student whose rare exposure to coercive rules sharply contrasts with his or her unregulated, arbitrary lifestyle perceives rules in school also as coercive and perceives cooperation with rules as *conformity.*

Rewards Considered Bribery and Barter

Exchange of rewards for behavior already poses unusual difficulties for many urban adolescents. Social problems in their lives abound with unclear solutions for teachers that limit the value of behavioral interventions (Kunkel, 1983). Misperception of rewards as "finders keepers" also challenges pristine uses of principles of behavior; this is because rewards are not functional, but competitive things. As such, street-thinking configures reinforcers as *objects of trade.* The view of reinforcers as "barter" or "bribery" for behaviors means, strictly speaking, equal exchange between consequences and behaviors. For example, students offered checkmarks as tokens for in-seat behaviors may object to "tokens" as being insubstantial and unequal in weight to the effort of appropriate sitting. They fail to see tokens as reinforcing symbols delaying the bigger payoff. Payoffs are expected immediately and must be commensurate barter for efforts made.

The major problem with "barter and bribery" mentality is student distrust. Juvenile criminals, particularly, develop suspicious behaviors socially validated by avoiding mistakes such as police arrest. They are unreceptive to kindness and unconditional gestures. Treats, gifts, and even friendships undergo scrutiny for questionable motives underlying a surface sweetness. Juvenile offenders ultimately trust no one and consequently are dubious about reinforcers that teachers give in class. Prizes, tokens, even class privileges clearly earned for the paranoid student's in-class participation are refused unless there are "no strings attached." Rewards are perceived as obligating the student to unwanted, compulsory actions. He or she may feel manipulated and recoil with defensively hostile protestations about abuse of rewards and exploitation of the classroom.

Punishment Perceived as Learning

One of the strangest, but assuredly most serious, cultural artifacts on contingencies is the belief that punishment promotes learning. Effects of punishment on behavior abound in the behavioral research literature (e.g., Boe & Church, 1968). Among its empirically prominent effects include avoidance and escape behaviors and aggression. Urban students may regard avoidance and escape behaviors as insightful and prudent behaviors. Perceptive students alert to dangerous predators or police surveillance may avoid arrest and continue illegal activities such as drug selling, theft and larceny, or writing graffiti. Likewise, aggressive students outwardly repel predators and not only retain their street reputation but also advance through the unwritten hierarchy of control over other students.

Punishment, in other words, *is misconstrued as guiding students through the concourse of unpredictable, hostile conflicts monopolizing their lives.* Environments replete with drive-by shootings, fights, drug use, rape, and crime are evocative signals for aggression and escape. Dougherty et al. (1998) recently supported this claim by experimentally showing that provocation and escape from provocation are necessary conditions for the occurrence and maintenance of aggressive behaviors. By analogy, students provoked by hostile peers may react swiftly and aggressively both as a causal effect of the provoker and to escape from the provoker. A bullied student may launch into a fight hoping to scare off his or her challenger and simultaneously to terminate future conflicts with the challenger. His or her victory glorifies the function of aggression. In this respect, aggression and escape behavior become respectable and favorable skills culled from punishment.

Nongenerality of Training Goals

School-based behavioral plans serve several reasons besides ameliorating student behavior. First is to relieve classroom disruption. But the second and more important goal is effecting systemic changes among high-risk students. Programs designed to promote transfer of skills from the original training environment in one classroom into another classroom and across home and school settings achieve powerful results, whereas programs with limited generality that benefit students in only one classroom or in one setting risk poor control over misbehavior; they require multiple interventions in every classroom. Poor behavior control is a phenomenon traditionally blamed on methodological imprecision such as trainer bias, inconsistent procedures, and intrusion of other variables (e.g., Johnston & Pennypacker, 1980). Thus far, discussion has focused on these pitfalls. Another methodological reason for nongenerality is apparent when training goals implemented for the classroom are inapplicable outside the classroom due to evocative and repertoire-altering effects (Michael, 1983) and field-integrative effects (Kantor, 1970; Ruben, 1983, 1986).

Evocative effects differ from repertoire-altering effects in terms of causal variables. Behaviors changed primarily due to antecedents such as discriminative cues are controlled by evocative effects. Middle school students may look at the hall clock or their watch to pace movement and prevent tardiness in between class-rooms. *Repertoire-altering effects* indicate that the primary causal factor is not ante-cedents but the consequences predictably produced by behavior, in this case tardiness. Late arrivals may get demerits, loss of privileges, or in-school detention. These factors alone constitute one-fourth of learning and generality. The remain-ing three-fourths of conditioning includes covariation of several factors such as socioculture, family history, states of motivation, and interrelationship among be-haviors inside and outside the school training environment. This interdependency between multiple variables constitutes a *field of the student's life context from which to predict the potency or impotence of learned behaviors.*

Field-integrative parameters advance the boundaries of traditional behavioral methodology. It asks both the standard question, Why does a student display this behavior? and the unconventional question, What factors surround that student's life from birth until present causing him or her to show this behavior? Without knowing the latter, behavioral methods cannot fully engineer evocative- and re-sponse-altering effects with stable, long-term outcomes. The following training problems show that critical field-integrative factors are missing and consequently prevent generality of skill learning.

Training Goals Are Inconsistent with Home Goals

One recurrent flaw is that school-based goals are diametrically opposite to home-based goals. For example, students enriched with in-class study habits may face incredible resistance by parents who demand their child hold a full work schedule outside school due to family financial constraints. Eight-hour shift jobs covering 30 to 40 hours a week eliminate reasonable homework time and eliminate appropriate study habits. Differential goals extinguish not only school-taught skills but the enthusiastic motivation emanating from earning passing or even high grades using those study skills.

Training Goals Presuppose Incentives That Are Nonexistent at Home

The assumption exists that school and home environments are equal. However, experience proves this assumption wrong when teachers employ incentives not replicable in the student's home life. Social reinforcers such as "catharsis" or talk-ing heart-to-heart with teachers, for example, may be desirable. Opportunities for open discussion accelerate students' in-class appropriate peer contact and signifi-cantly improve their interpersonal communication skills. Sadly, cathartic dialogue is a scarce reinforcer and found only at school. Absence of the reinforcer at home profoundly produces two effects. First, it diminishes an incentive to earn the rein-forcer, and, second, it also disables transference of interpersonally appropriate conversation skills. Alternatively, the healthy, expressive student at school is quiet or reverts to using profanity at home.

Training Goals Control for Social Variables Unlike at Home

A sad, but true, reality between school and urban home settings is variability. School settings can artificially control extraneous variables that contaminate classroom procedures and retard skill acquisition. Like a laboratory, insulated training protects students from disturbing distractions and competing responses. Outside this bubble, students inevitably get deluged with a torrent of distractions that gradually weaken responses until responses are decomposed. Female students, for example, may deflect a persistent male predator at school supported by teachers and administrators punishing the predator. After school hours, that predator stalks his female prey without safeguards conveniently in place protecting her from unwanted contact.

Training Goals Are Behavior-Isolative, Not Behavior-Integrative

A serious shortcoming of behavior methods in school involves restricted focus on isolated behaviors rather than integrative behaviors. *Behavior-isolative* approaches teach new skills under singular training conditions as in one classroom or one skill per consequence. Even schoolwide contingencies may track one or possibly two behaviors (e.g., politeness, anger control) using identical consequences in each classroom. *Behavior-integrative* approaches, by contrast, construct skills with multiply diverse contingencies engineered to boost and secure generality across many settings (Delprato, 1987; Delprato & McGlynn, 1986). Diversely trained skills are flexible and adapt readily to unforeseen changes in the natural urban environment. Changes such as eviction from home, food shortages, or investigative visits from Child Protective Services may result in a student's temporary placement in foster homes. Students clobbered by these frantic lifestyle problems recover quickly from defeat and retain school-based skills despite wide variance in settings.

Training Goals Are Teacher-Directed, Not Self-Regulatory

A final setback for generality is skills designed with teacher-directed versus self-regulatory learning. Teacher-directed skills largely require instructors to implement and oversee the contingency, including troubleshooting defects in the system. Students who rely on teachers or school support staff may produce impressive gains and automatically appear self-motivated to carry over skills into nonschool environments. However, "self-motivation" presents a problem. It is a reified concept based on false assumptions that student progress inherently resides *in the person* and can be transported to new places like transporting luggage. Motivation, unfortunately, is not inside the person or automatically transportable across settings (e.g., Ruben & Ruben, 1987). It is *in the environment and requires that a student interact with events conducive to learning.*

Motivation can be developed in any environment using self-regulatory methods. Self-regulatory systems teach from the outset the self-directive and self-supportive procedures students need to remain on-task without teacher supervision; students also learn to discern signs of skill deterioration. Students observing their own regression implement steps that avert potential problems and revert to stable skills using self-reinforcement. Motivation in this respect derives from students' success at *operating on the natural environment to produce changes duplicating the school environment.*

PARAMETERS OF EFFECTIVE BEHAVIORAL PROGRAMS

Severity of procedural flaws besieges the standard behavior modification program in school for reasons ranging from teacher bias and cultural irrelevance of contingencies to nongenerality of training results. School personnel sensitive to these defects remarkably rebound with innovative remedies sharpening in-class programs. For example, current programs now incorporate more comprehensive functional assessment of training variables (Broussard & Northrup, 1997). Programs also insightfully consider "collateral" effects of training that include targeted as well as nontargeted behaviors (e.g., Martella et al., 1995). Together, these significant advances eliminate many methodological pitfalls described earlier and provide students impetus for stronger behavior changes.

Just the same, school methods fail not because programs are always structurally defective or principles of conditioning are too narrow. Faults arise due to improperly designing the methodology to suit urban demography. Urbanity demands a rethinking of controlling variables chosen and implemented in behavioral programs. Relevant variables applied at the outset of training may accomplish two goals. First is to inoculate students from hazards of home life variability. Second is to minimize inconsistency between training (school) and natural settings (home). Procedural changes described later can exert realistic control over generalizability of behavior and thereby enhance school interventions.

Procedures for Generalizable Behavioral Urban Programs

Programming generalization is not a new phenomenon. Behavioral researchers long since established valid approaches for instilling skills across a labyrinth of environments (Stokes & Baer, 1977). In altering addictive repertoires, response generalization even includes highly systematic and self-regulatory safeguards to prevent relapse (Marlatt & Gordon, 1985; Ruben, 1993b). The ubiquity of generalization thus verifies why schools prefer behavioral over nonbehavioral interventions. In urban school settings, however, rules for programming generalization are less known. Informing teachers of these rules thus is essential. Following are revised procedures for enhancing generalization among urban students.

Acquisition of Survival Adaptive Behaviors

One of the major transitions assuring behavior continuity is use of survival adaptive behaviors. Adaptive behaviors consist of three components. First are assertiveness interpersonal skills. These skills enable students to refuse negative peer influence and persist with their needs against impulsive temptations. Second are variability skills. Students deliberately learn to adapt to unexpected or bizarre changes in life circumstances unaffecting their new skills. For example, students learn study habits resistant to intrusion of noise, family interruptions, and project delays. With practice, students can study for a test while their family is louder, rudely interrupting them or when delayed by making dinner or working a job.

A third component is accepting procedural imperfection. Students are taught immediately that skills fluctuate in cyclical spirals and may not always remain pristine or productive. This prepares students to handle minor setbacks. Acceptance of limitations also includes awareness that preferable reinforcers may be absent and prompt creative alternatives to choose a new pool of reinforcers.

Acquisition of Self-Regulated Behaviors

Generalization critically employs strategies for students to self-operate a contingency without the life support of school staff. Self-regulatory methods are manifold and typically entail four components. First is the conceptual understanding of antecedents, concurrent behaviors, consequences, establishing operations, or any other variables predictably causal in reproducing the skills. Second is for students to simulate self-regulatory activity within school settings where the entire duration from onset to self-delivery of reinforcers transpires without teacher input. Third, graded, in-school, self-regulatory performance prepares students to duplicate the exact sequence of steps in several different external environments, from home, to work, to recreational settings. Fourth, students receive troubleshooting skills enabling their own early detection of procedural problems and ability to rapidly design efficient remedies. Methods of self-repair particularly emphasize the importance of remaining calm, confident, and perseverant in restoring an operational contingency.

Programmed Transferability Across People and Places

Survival-adaptive skills described earlier alluded to this procedure. Training must include deliberate practice of skills across a wide variety of people and places within the student's natural environment. For example, speaking in correct English (and no profanity) may poorly occur in social or home settings where peers and family members are illiterate or criticize the student for correctly worded sentences. Uneducated urban adults may criticize their articulate children for sounding "too adult and thus disrespectful." Facing this oppressive obstacle, students must use diplomatic explanations to ingratiate their parents while maintaining the frequency and topography of their improved language skills.

Training in Self-Generative Reward Systems

A common failure in programming generality is not preselecting a vast collection of reinforcers obtainable by students outside the training environment. Reinforcers used in school provided initial pedagogy. Instructionally, they generated and kept behavior levels at a regularly high pace without drops to baseline levels. Teachers administered the vast array of reinforcers and replenished exhausted supplies before students' behaviors fluctuated. Teacher-generated reinforcers guaranteed, in other words, that contingencies flowed uninterruptedly and met the diversely changing needs of student learners.

By contrast, student-generative reward systems depend on learners' finding and replenishing their own reservoir of reinforcers. Selection of reinforcers may seem obvious. Either students can replicate reinforcers that were effective at school and thus control stability at home, or, more practically speaking, rein-forcer selection may include resources that are *functional*. Functional reinforcers resist extinction longer because they (1) already exist in the student's natural set-ting, (2) routinely are used on a daily basis, (3) pair with numerous other reinforers, rendering them generalized conditioned reinforcers, and (4) appear noncompetitive and unlimited.

Functional reinforcers include a showcase of activities and habits embedded in the student's lifestyle and economically feasible. For example, as a routine after school, a student eats a snack while watching 30 minutes of television. Afterward, he contacts his friends by phone to see who is available to play "hoops" (pickup game of basketball). The reinforcers ensconced in his routines include (1) eating a snack, (2) television viewing for 30 minutes, (3) calling friends, and (4) playing basketball. Potentially, one or several of these inherently structured reinforcers can be reorganized as consequences that follow homework completion or test-study behaviors. He can first spend 30 minutes finishing math or reviewing his social studies for tomorrow's quiz; then he can eat a snack, watch television, call friends, or play basketball. Rearrangement of existing reinforcers is facile and increases the probability of self-regulatory control of contingencies with moderate risk of pro-gram failure.

Sensitization of Conformity, Cooperation, and Compassion

Finally, contingency management is an effective process only if three condi-tions are present. The first two already received discussion pertaining to proce-dural accuracy and generality of training results. A third condition is having students who *care*. Behaviorally speaking, *caring* represents a unique set of moral, ethical, and social behaviors largely controlled by both reinforcing and punish-ing consequences (Bijou, 1975; Ruben, 1987). Students showing *sensitivity and benevolence* may either attract praise and accolades for their compassion or repel friends and be criticized for appearing vulnerable and manipulable. Against fears of rejection, inner-city students may suppress, deny, or repudiate sensitive feel-ings to outwardly draw peer acceptance. Associate gang members, particularly, may disguise their cooperative or moralistic behaviors to prevent gang recruiters from ignoring them. Once they are "blessed-in" or "beaten-in," freshman gang members further depersonalize from caring. They assume a rebellious posture as accomplices to terroristic activities ranging from intimidation, to burglaries, to drive-by shootings.

Gang members or other hostile juveniles avoiding aversive peer reactions de-velop a callus against emotions. Their fiercely aggressive behaviors inhibit aware-ness of their own or another person's suffering, thereby removing remorseful thoughts and guilty feelings. Oppositional anger also displaces their self-caring and erases their motivation to improve behaviors. In school, disruptive teens ini-tially respond poorly to behavioral programs and perform poorly during later stages of self-regulatory training. Repeated failures at behavioral interventions are an abysmal process as students discretely fall through the cracks of the system and remain ignored and forgotten.

The solution clearly calls for restoration or construction of the student's sensitivity skills and forfeiting the futile behavioral program. One common method implemented before a behavioral plan begins is called *the sensitivity training package.* This package primarily consists of eight components sequentially taught using a psychoeducational format involving note taking, homework, tests, and mandatory in-class participation. Components cover (1) social alertness; (2) compassion and caring; (3) social skills; (4) impulse control; (5) overcoming high-risk thrill; (6) engaging in restitution; (7) relapse prevention; and (8) use of community resources. Lessons elaborate on practical, how-to skills demonstrated in vivo during the session and designed for application outside the school. The author, for example, currently employs sensitivity training with teen drug dealers and drug addicts ordered into groups by their parole officers. Probationers, like students, regard themselves as invincible until reconditioned to experience fear, love, and self-respect. Once these skills return, propensity to perform a in behavioral program is significantly higher.

CONCLUSIONS

Urban decay purportedly contributes to unmotivated juvenile delinquents, unaffectionately described as "losers" and "social derelicts." Many school personnel may even conclude they are not rehabilitative. Beliefs that inner-city children have untreatable polymorbidity emanate from reports of special education and regular classroom instructors who are tired of using worn-out, recycled versions of behavioral methods and who watch minimal progress vanish once students leave the classroom and return home. Futility results not only from antiquated methodology but also from subjectively biased teachers who, admittedly, exhaust their optimism after repeatedly suffering one student disaster after another. As juvenile crimes increase, teacher fears abound that aggressive students will become uncontrollable and devour classroom control.

This chapter, like the chapters following it, disputes this thesis of futility. Behavioral programs fail not only because today's students are worse but because the technology to cure them is old and requires updating for contingency management and program generalization. Revisions for advancing this technology are offered on enhancing response generalization from school to home environments. Toward this end, confidence restored in behavioral procedures may motivate teachers, as it does students, to undertake innovative programming against a backdrop of urban oppression.

Part II

Current Advances in Urban Behavioral Management

ALTERNATIVE SYSTEMS FOR ASSESSMENT AND GRADING STUDENTS

Nancy R. Macciomei

In recent years, there has been an increasing emphasis on identifying appropriate classroom assessment methods and practices used with high-risk children. This emphasis includes a widespread interest in traditional and alternative forms of assessment used with high-risk students in urban settings who exhibit behavior problems. These students have long histories of academic failure resulting in a lower self-esteem and causing a continued lack of motivation in an academic setting. The common denominator of these children is their deficits in learning, their vulnerability to develop a breakdown in their motivation, and a continued cycle of school failure (Licht & Dweck, 1984). Repeated failures cause children to view themselves as having no control over long-term achievement outcomes as well as daily classroom performance (Durante, 1993; Mercer & Mercer, 1993).

Hearne (1992) affirms that the tendency of high-risk, urban children to attribute school failure to uncontrollable causes is related to their school grades, which are based on traditional classroom assessment methods. Selby and Murphy (1992) also support the research stating that present models of assessment have contributed to academic failure. In regular classes across the nation, students often become subject to evaluation in terms of letter grading and standards against which they failed in the first place. Traditional classroom assessment practices often reflect a limited range of evaluative practices available for these students. Bennett and Hawkins (1993) state that traditional assessment practices emphasize just two abilities: recall of facts and concepts and solving short, well-defined problems. These abilities are not representative of the range of abilities required for academic success for elementary and secondary urban students.

Alternatively, models of assessment more accurately and reliably discerning academic progress in high-risk, urban students require measurement of behaviors atypical in most curriculum assessment. This chapter first examines pitfalls in traditional assessment in juxtaposition to recommended revisions. Adopting these revisions, although seemingly arduous, provides educators with two sources of control. One is a predictor of student academic growth inclusive of existing obstacles impairing learning. Second are reliability and validity of the class curricula in generating acquisition of relevant versus irrelevant educational skills.

TRADITIONAL ASSESSMENTS

There are several traditional assessment and evaluation methods currently used in classrooms across America. None of the common methods of traditional classroom assessment, including traditional scoring and grading practices, address the issues of motivation, authentic growth and development, and self-reflection. These variables are needed to work with high-risk, urban children. The current classroom assessment system taps only a small part of the basic content and curriculum (McClure, 1992).

According to a U.S. Federal Appeals Court ruling (*Wynne v. Tufts University*, 1990), traditional assessments such as multiple-choice testing may discriminate against the rights of students with specific learning disabilities. A U.S. Court of Appeals for the First Circuit ruled that the requirement that college students with specific learning disabilities take multiple-choice tests may violate their civil rights. This ruling came about as a result of a lawsuit from a dyslexic student at Tufts University. The student charged that the school had discriminated against him because of his disability when it refused to provide a test that did not use multiple-choice questions. The alleged discrimination stems not from the particular skills required, such as the ability to work with complex data, but from the method by which Tuft University measured that ability (p. 18). The ruling continued to state that Tufts University has offered no evidence explaining why multiple-choice examinations test students' ability to assimilate, interpret, and analyze complex written material (Jaschik, 1990). This case may have broad implications for future assessment of our urban, high-risk students. The ruling and those like it may force educators and administrators to consider alternative methods of assessment.

McClure (1992) states that not only do traditional classroom tests fail to measure achievement in the more complicated concepts students are learning, but they also distort the educational system in fundamental ways. First, tests (e.g., end-of-chapter tests, end-of-course tests, curriculum-referenced tests) influence curriculum decisions and limit the pedagogy. Second, they give the illusion of objectivity and fairness. They tend to take assessment out of the flow of activity of the classroom and position it in an artificial environment for a specified period of time. Third, they make the classroom assessment issue one of reduction, reducing learning and performance to numbers and grades. Researchers opposed to traditional assessment practices (Resnick & Resnick, 1985; Shepard, 1991; Wolf et al., 1991) state that traditional classroom tests may promote skills that are inconsistent with learning and demonstrating problem-solving skills. The U.S. Federal Appeals Court ruling, coupled with the body of research opposing traditional assessment practices, urges teachers to implement alternative assessments, or, at least, to supplement traditional practices with alternative measures of student performance.

- ### Traditional Test Formats

Traditional classroom assessment includes essay tests, oral questioning, and objective tests such as true/false, fill in the blanks (with or without word banks), matching, or multiple-choice tests. Success on objective tests requires not only an organized plan of study and memorization skills but also efficient gathering of materials to be studied (Cohen, 1986).

Essay testing is used to assess thinking skills and mastery of a body of knowledge. Scoring may be subjective, based on an evaluation of understanding and composition skills (Rothman & Cohen, 1988). The advantage of essay testing is that it provides an opportunity to measure complex cognitive outcomes. There are, however, potential sources of inaccurate evaluation for urban children who are poorly motivated and exhibit behavior problems. First, these students may possess poor writing skills and therefore produce poorly written compositions. Their knowledge of subject content may be limited due to disruptions in the learning process. Second, essay testing, when scored on writing proficiency that includes memorization of facts integrated into the text, may be an inappropriate assessment tool. These disadvantages are only some of many practical reasons to seek alternative testing methods.

Oral questioning, when implemented as open-ended questions, can be used to monitor or evaluate student performance. Stiggins (1987) asserts that oral questioning often does not measure knowledge gained through instruction. Although an advantage of oral questioning is to integrate assessment and instruction, the potential sources of inaccurate assessment, such as lack of willingness to respond in class, too few questions for each individual, or intimidation from questioning by teacher, may outweigh the advantages.

Objective testing, the most common traditional form of assessment, includes multiple-choice, true/false, fill-in-the-blank, and matching test items. The purpose of objective testing is to sample knowledge with maximum efficiency and reliability (Farr, 1991). The major focus of objective testing has been on efficiency. Objective tests can be administered utilizing many items per unit of testing time. There are potential sources of inaccurate evaluation due to problems with test construction, such as poorly written items, an emphasis on instant recall of facts, poor test-taking skills, and a failure to sample representatively. Although objective testing may be efficient, it does not measure students' ability to integrate information using an ongoing method of assessment.

The most common traditional assessment used in the classroom is the multiple-choice test. The greatest concern with multiple-choice testing is that students are not required to develop responses. Rather, they merely select an answer choice from several that have already been constructed for them. Farr (1991) states that educators have long recognized that it is a far different matter to write a complete sentence with correct punctuation than it is to answer a question that asks which of four punctuation marks should be placed at the end of a sentence. Critics such as Wolf et al. (1991) claim that multiple-choice tests are culturally biased, irrelevant, and poorly aligned with the curriculum and measure the wrong things (lower-order versus higher-order thinking). Traditional classroom tests appear to teach skills, such as guessing and quick response recognition finding, that are inconsistent with learning and demonstrating problem solving. Educators today maintain that the use of short answer or multiple-choice tests runs counter to the development of those critical thinking, problem-solving strategies so necessary in a changing world (Resnick & Resnick, 1985).

Advantages and Disadvantages of Traditional Grading Practices

Traditional grading practices, such as assigning letter grades (A, B, C, D, E, and F), are among the most salient experiences of school life. *They have been characterized as the basic currency of our educational system* (Deutsch, 1979, p. 391). Then, too, they are a major problem area in school for all school-age students. The major problem inherent in using the same grading system for all students is that the letters or numbers can mean different things for different students. For example, grades may be assigned to offer motivation for some students and as a quantitative device to summarize student performance for others. Bruder (1993) stated that when determining grades, teachers often take into consideration variables (e.g., ability levels, disabling conditions, behavior problems) other than those directly related to the evaluation of task performance. Terwillinger (1971) provided a framework for the discussion of letter grades by stating that there were four reasons for assigning grades:

- Motivational tools
- An aid in guiding students' career planning
- Administrative purposes
- Informational devices to summarize student performance for parents and students

Although these reasons appear valid, they are dependent on the extent to which grades are accurate assessments of a students ability. Urban students exhibiting intermittent or continuous disruptive behavior experience information-processing deficits that affect their ability to demonstrate content knowledge. Therefore, grades cannot be assumed to be accurate assessments for this population. Letter grades and numerical grades may provide misleading information to the school, parents, and students.

An extremely important factor in the grading process is that negative characteristics of our urban students may cause the teacher to develop a negative attitude toward those students' academic potential. If teachers place undue emphasis on the effects of a particular behavior problem or inappropriate social skills, they may be unable to objectively evaluate students' academic performances.

The issue of grades with urban students who typically demonstrate behavior problems is a central concern. The use of conventional grades for these students would appear to be of little use and convey minimal information in order to plan future lessons. According to Bennett and Hawkins (1993), it is time to go beyond traditional classroom assessment grades, which overemphasize facts and instant recall; rather, educators should develop methods for assessing complex knowledge and performances. Current literature (Chapman, 1988; Shephard & Smith, 1988; Valencia, 1990) suggests that alternative classroom assessment systems are needed to measure and promote motivation as well as the individual educational goals that are known to be critical to students' success in academic achievement and behavior management.

ALTERNATIVE ASSESSMENTS

Assessment is the process of gathering information, using appropriate tools and techniques (Hargrove & Poteet, 1984, p. 5). When assessing any student, teachers must keep in mind that they are dealing with a whole human being who is more important than the skills they are trying to assess (Poteet et al., 1993), meaning that emphasis must be given to various aspects of the student's life that influence behaviors and functioning in the classroom. Racial and cultural mores, family expectations, personal interests, and the overall home situation including family expectations—these numerous factors all contribute to the educator's ability to make sense and fully assess the total person. With this in mind, consider some assessment strategies that enable you to pinpoint the learning needs of your students. The approach to assessment relies on three basic diagnostic skills which are taken from Hargrove and Poteet (1984).

Assessment strategies use the skills of diagnostic looking, diagnostic asking, and diagnostic listening. *Diagnostic looking* refers to the observation of a student's behavior and an attempt to explain why a particular behavior occurs. It involves the critical investigation of anything that can be analyzed visually, such as work sheets, written responses, and so on. *Diagnostic asking* is the use of questioning to reveal possible reasons for error patterns or to pinpoint answers to the teacher's diagnostic questions. The teacher may develop a hypothesis about the cause of the student's lack of achievement or observed error patterns. In many cases, the causes relate to factors not immediately seen, such as prerequisite skills or possibly a delay in language development. As the information is acquired, the hypothesis may be either accepted or rejected, and other hypotheses developed. *Diagnostic listening* is the careful evaluation of what the student actually says compared to what the student may imply by his or her responses. The teacher or diagnostician uses the three assessment skills to determine as many learning characteristics about the student as possible. Poteet et al. (1993) states the following six learning characteristics to determine through assessment:

1. Curriculum skills known and unknown.
2. Preferred environment for learning (large/small group, one-to-one, formal/informal setting).
3. Preferred instructional personnel (teacher, peer/cross-age tutor, paraprofessional, parent).
4. Modality preferences for learning.

5. Thinking style (approach to the task, learning and memory strategies used).

6. Effect, if any, of emotions on learning.

Becoming familiar with several assessment tools and techniques, educators can select those that best suit the purposes of their assessment of each student. Assessment results provide the database to make informed, instructional decisions. An educational program developed for an individual student should provide a specific set of learning experiences that will allow progress through the curriculum at the student's optimum level and pace.

Content, materials, and methods should be planned in order to ensure a high probability of skill mastery. Methods and materials with which a student has previously experienced success may be considered in developing the prescriptive program. Without modification, no methods should be included. The combination of the particular skill content, methods selected, and materials chosen produces an educational program specific to a student's needs (Choate & Miller, 1992).

Assessment results also dictate program content. The content areas in which a student's skills are found to be minimal provide the core content for that student's individual programming. Walberg (1990) stated that teaching students what they already know and teaching them what they are yet incapable of learning are equally wasteful practices and may even be harmful to motivation. However, mastered tasks related to deficit areas must also be included in the program to avoid overwhelming the student (Ysseldyke & Algozzine, 1990). Content emphasis is determined by ranking the importance to a student's progress of identified target skill areas. Within each area, rank specific subskills according to orderly sequence as well as relative importance. Several sources provide the data for this ranking, including objective evaluation of assessment results, teacher and system policy and priorities, and their relative significance to student and parent. A practical ranking of skills, subskills, tasks, and strategies by priority should emerge from use of alternative assessments with content emphasis.

Gable et al. (1991) define alternative assessment as the process of understanding the performance of students in terms of their current ecology or learning environment. The purpose is perceived as the method of matching student competencies to the demands of the learning environment within the instructional curriculum. Alternative assessment methods may be the link to effective instruction and behavior management. Bauer (1993) asserts that alternative assessment provides a more authentic and valid portrait of a student's competencies, helping to acquire a clear understanding of what has been learned. Alternative assessment represents knowledge of real experiences drawn from authentic performance tasks. This type of assessment provides the process of ongoing insight into how children think, interact, and behave developmentally.

The key part of alternative assessment is developing tasks that enable students to use and demonstrate a broad range of abilities. Alternative methods must accurately measure and promote the complex thinking and learning goals that are known to be critical to students' academic success and reduced school-failure experiences. Two approaches to alternative assessments are performance-based assessments and curriculum-based assessments. In these approaches, judgments about students' achievement are based on their performances of daily tasks and selections of work over time.

Performance-Based Assessment

Alternative classroom assessments should be designed to enable students to use and demonstrate a broad range of abilities. Due to the wide range of deficits in reading and written expression, high-risk students may require an assessment method that encompasses their varied ability levels as well as their strengths and weaknesses within the testing domain. Performance tasks should be complex enough to engage students in critical thinking and open-ended enough to encourage varied abilities and learning styles.

Performance-based assessment refers to the process of evaluating a student's skills by asking the student to perform tasks that require those skills. Bennett et al. (1991) state that a performance task can (1) allow examination of the process used as well as the answer or finished project, (2) be given to an individual, small group, an entire class, several classes, a school, or any other group, and (3) document, through observation records or students' products, accomplishments not revealed by traditional classroom tasks or tests. According to Wiggins (1991), the key words in performance-based assessment are *authentic* and *engaging*. "Authentic" refers to the autonomous, independent action of each student. This includes the basic knowledge, skills, and interpretive powers being acquired by students in their pursuit of learning. "Engaging" refers to intrinsic responses toward problems that require students to use a multitude of intelligences and their full repertoire of knowledge and skill to form critical thinking skills.

Wiggins (1991) and the Connecticut State Department of Education developed a set of dimensions desirable for implementing performance tasks:

1. *Essential.* Tangential: Each performance task fits into the core curriculum, representing a major theme, and important concepts of a particular discipline are being assessed.

2. *Authentic.* Contrived: Each performance task uses processes appropriate to the discipline and involves problems in real-life contexts.

3. *Integrative.* Disjointed: Each performance task requires students to put together a variety of essential skills, knowledge, concepts, writing, reasoning, and so on.

4. *Rich.* Superficial: Each performance task requires a variety of answers or means of solving the problem as well as leading to other problems/questions.

5. *Engaging.* Uninteresting: Each performance task is thought-provoking and fosters persistence; students will value the outcome of the task.

6. *Active.* Passive: Each performance task requires the student to be the worker, interact with other students, and construct meaning as well as deepens understanding.

The advantages of performance-based assessment, state Davey and Rindone (1990), include (1) an opportunity to display all of students' ability, not just speed and accuracy; (2) more creative activities to work on; (3) opportunities to do their own organizing and thinking; and (4) participation in real tasks that offer engaging contexts that may enhance motivation. Advantages for teachers include assessment that does not interrupt student learning but occurs within the instructional program, such as increased information of higher quality about students' understanding; ability within the curriculum for instructional decisions about student errors or misconceptions; and better assessment of strengths and weaknesses of the instructional process. There are also advantages for parents and administrators, including examples of real performance by students, comprehensive evaluation of students' ability to utilize their understanding of curriculum, and evaluation of outcomes of basic curricular programs.

Assessment of subject domains is a major purpose for the implementation of performance-based assessment. Many of the inadequacies and limitations of current assessment procedures can be eliminated if focus is on instruction and teacher decision making using curriculum-referenced approaches such as *curriculum-based assessment*. Curriculum-based assessment, like performance-based assessment, has been proposed as another alternative to traditional classroom assessment.

Curriculum-Based Assessment

Both regular and special education teachers need assessment approaches to determine the best instructional practices to use with all students. One very effective alternative assessment for high-risk children is curriculum-based assessment.

Curriculum-based assessment (CBA) is the process of determining students' instructional needs within a curriculum by directly assessing specific curriculum skills (Poteet et al., 1993). A variety of models of CBA tends to emphasize measurement that is brief, frequent, and based on the students' classroom curriculum and that can be used to monitor instructional progress and effectiveness. Used to define, instruct, and measure academic growth, this technique is directly based on academic behavior and provides data on teaching/learning events within the classroom. There are five reasons for using CBA as an alternative assessment method in the urban classroom:

First, CBA helps teachers determine what to teach. In most school systems, the curriculum has been developed by school personnel and parents to represent necessary and desirable skills for students to learn. CBA is implemented to see that the students master the curriculum content. Those skills that have not been mastered receive priority for instruction.

Second, CBA is efficient, simple, easily understood, inexpensive, and correlates with educational decisions. These factors are a clear advantage of CBA. The use of frequent assessment allows progress toward mastery and attainment of short-term instructional objectives specified in the student's individualized educational plan (IEP). Charting is also an appealing method of presenting achievement progress to parents.

Third, CBA facilitates evaluation of student progress and program effectiveness. Intermittent monitoring, such as keeping a daily or weekly log of a student's knowledge of basic curriculum skills, allows the teacher to evaluate progress on student cumulated knowledge. Teachers accomplish this by using a mastery learning approach and setting a certain percentage of correct skills as the criterion of mastery. Administrators and parents find this approach to evaluation easy to understand. CBA gives precise information for determining which approach facilitates better achievement.

Fourth, curriculum-based assessment is both valid and reliable, a definite advantage over performance-based assessment. Since CBA uses materials from the student's curriculum, content validity is assured. Salvia and Ysseldyke (1984) point out that since time measurements are brief, repeated samplings are easily obtained, giving increased reliability to estimates of the student's performance.

Fifth, curriculum-based assessment increases student achievement. Pophan (1985) asserts that when what is taught becomes what is assessed, measures of student achievement increase. He points out that if the assessment tools used are criterion-related tests that have been constructed to enhance instructional decision making, then the testing program drives the instructional program.

Although alternative assessments such as CBA and performance-based assessments have their merits, Wesson and King (1992) state that *effective alternative assessments must help to provide a more balanced analysis incorporating more than just evaluating instructional plans.* Another major concern about both alternative assessments is that teachers must be able to record progress accurately over time to make decisions about instruction. In addition to stated problems with traditional measures, assessment for instructional decision making must keep abreast of new ideas about curriculum and instruction.

The direction of assessment is to make use of more instructionally relevant types of assessment that will also incorporate components that assess areas of deficits, including self-regulation, self-evaluation, and self-reflection. Alternative assessments are more capable of addressing these areas, needed by students exhibiting behavior problems, because they promote participation in setting goals and judgment of progress toward goals. Effective alternative assessment must also help to improve areas such as intrinsic motivation and student-initiated questioning and problem solving. Alternative assessments such as perfomance-based assessment and curriculum-based assessment thus have clear advantages for high-risk, urban children. However, they may not adequately address the goal-setting and self-reflection factors that interact to make each student's needs unique (Smith, 1991).

Assessment of specific curriculum-based skills comprises the application of skills to everyday, authentic life situations, not just skills used today but skills projected over time. This represents the underlying purpose of the assessment. Fuchs and Deno (1991) state that measuring long-term goals rather than short-term objectives should be the focus.

On a more practical level, the appropriate procedure to determine the instructional needs of students is to review the basic curriculum. For example, if a curriculum indicates that the student should be able to read at sight the 220 Dolch basic words, then you would present each of the words on a flash card and ask the student to read them. Since direct assessment leads to direct instruction, the student's instructional needs would not be what the student can read, but rather *what the student cannot read*, that is, the unknown words on the Dolch list (Poteet et al. 1993).

The role of the curriculum in the educational process is extremely important to the education of any student. The most important way a curriculum functions is by representing the logical source for both assessment data and programming data. Before examining the ways in which a curriculum can be adjusted to accommodate the learning needs of individual students, alternative assessements must provide reliable and valid information. In addition, a key part of successful and effective alternative assessment is developing tasks that will enable each student to use and demonstrate a broad range of abilities. Successful tasks should be complex enough to engage students in real thinking and performances, open-ended enough to encourage different learning styles, yet sufficiently constrained to permit reliable scoring, allow for easy collection of data, and exemplify authentic work in the classroom.

Appropriate and valid alternative assessments must contribute to the fundamental purpose of measurement—the improvement of instruction and learning toward effective growth and development. Rogers and Saklofske (1985) support the notion that interventions such as alternative classroom assessments may also alter inappropriate behaviors and increase self-esteem. One method of alternative assessment that holds promise for fostering positive motivation, deterring school failure, and focusing on self-regulated academic achievement is portfolio assessment.

Portfolio Assessment

Portfolio assessment (PA) is a method of assessment that is used to evaluate students' ability, knowledge base, skills, attitudes, and dispositions through students' work gathered over a period of time (Meyer, 1992). In general, PA is a term used to describe data that are gathered systematically for the purpose of making educational decisions. PA attempts to provide extended records of student performance, to motivate students to choose and reflect on their efforts, and to provide opportunities for teacher–student conferencing designed to enhance individual growth and development. The portfolio is a collection of documents, written assignments, projects, and reflections assembled over a period of time by a student demonstrating his or her competence, knowledge, skills, abilities, and dispositions in relevant fields. Wolf (1992) states that portfolio assessment is singled out as an appropriate assessment for high-risk children because it requires self-reflection and one-on-one conferencing on the significance or contribution of the students' daily performance tasks.

Poteet et al. (1993) assert that PA is an effective method for systematizing and expanding the process of analyzing samples of students' class work. They add, however, that enhancing the value of PA as a formalized assessment technique may involve restructuring. Such restructuring may include preselecting content and spacing assignments to display progress, selecting tasks to include current levels of performance, analyzing both error and success patterns, evaluating performance of the portfolio content with each student, and planning subsequent instruction and assignments on the basis of the assessed performance. Portfolios also present opportunities for teachers to guide students toward self-assessment and independent learning.

Effective use of portfolio assessment requires that each portfolio be developed to serve a specified purpose. Research revealed that PA is one of the most meaningful ways to utilize several assessment approaches in tracking students and assisting children with behavior problems. The underlying assumption is that judgments based on portfolios are more reliable and valid because the evidence is more inclusive and comprehensive (Grady, 1992).

Portfolio assessment also addresses the specific needs of the nation's urban children who demonstrate a short attention span, lack of motivation, and mild to serious behavior problems. As discussed in Chapter 1, there is a wide cultural diversity in the pace and style of development among urban school-age children. By personalizing assessment, portfolios create a structure for individualized learning. With PA, students are encouraged to revise their work and are motivated to take the initiative in conferring with the teacher and their peers. The students assume responsibility for their work and their learning. As Ringler (1992) suggests, data can be collected on an ongoing basis, and instructional decisions can be seen as a collaboration between teachers and learners as they actively evaluate what is being taught. Learners become self-critical, questioning their own learning and setting their own goal.

According to Farr (1991), portfolio collections serve as the foundation for teacher–student conferences, a vital component of portfolio assessment. Through conferencing students with behavior problems gain insight into how they operate in academic areas. Moreover, through conferences, learners participate in self-regulation and self-evaluation by taking risks with, and responsibility for, their learning. Students are encouraged to share what they know and understand about the subject matter; this exercise increases specific cognitive activities (e.g., reading, writing, social skills). PA also allows students to take a special role in the assessment process. Instead of making them the subjects of the examination, they are the designers of the assessment (McClure, 1992).

Researchers have come to recognize that *thinking about one's own thinking, or metacognition,* is an important element of learning. Portfolio assessment encourages metacognitive functions and students' reflections. Students are asked to systematically evaluate their learning on a particular project or across a set of tasks. This creates the opportunity for students to recognize, analyze, and discuss their thinking and learning. The process of collecting student work has the potential for both encouraging and documenting critical thinking, problem solving, and independent thinking. Portfolio assessment is an appropriate means of providing the link between instruction and assessment (Tierney, 1992).

Approaches to Scoring Portfolio Assessment

Several different approaches to scoring students' portfolio collections are currently in development. For example, analytic scales or rubrics are being tried in

Vermont and across the nation as a method of assessing selected key aspects of competent writing. These aspects include sentence variety, sense of personal expression, mechanics, fluency, organization, and skill with draft revision (Tierney et al., 1991). Arter and Spandel (1992) state that there are potential benefits for clear criteria in scoring procedures. Those who set the criteria must think very carefully about what they value in strong performance. This helps clarify instructional goals and expectations. Also, to the extent that criteria are shared, students are made part of the evaluation and receive the power that goes with that specialized knowledge—power to recognize strong performance, power to identify problems in weak performance, and power to use criteria to change and improve performance. Finally, clear criteria for scoring portfolio assessment are the basic means for one to judge performance on any level.

Most portfolios are composed of working files, tests, and best pieces of students' work. The teachers provide folders for students' working portfolios and time for students to add to, and organize, their work. The portfolios provide the context for an integrated set of assessment activities: student self-assessment, teacher–student conferencing, informal parent conferencing, and parent–administration assessment.

Several features distinguish PA from the other alternative assessment or traditional assessments discussed in this chapter. Portfolio assessment methods capture a richer array of what students know and can do. Current goals for students go beyond knowledge of facts and include such things as problem solving, critical thinking, lifelong learning of new information, and thinking independently. Goals also include dispositions such as persistence, flexibility, motivation, and self-confidence. Another feature is the process by which students produce work. Students monitor their own learning so they can adjust what they do when they perceive they are not understanding. A meaningful feature is that continuous information is provided on how students are doing in order to chronicle development, give effective feedback to them, and encourage them to observe their own growth. In this way, portfolio assessment methods thereby integrate assessment with instruction in a way consistent with both current theories of instruction and goals for our urban students.

4

Computer Technology for High-Risk Students

Nancy R. Macciomei and Gregg Byrum

Computer technology in our public schools has grown rapidly within the last 15 years. Research shows that almost every school in America uses computers to some extent. The use of peripherals, such as modems, is on the rise as well. However, growth in number *does not necessarily mean* that there is equity with availability and use of computers or that computers are improving student performance. For schools to get the most out of their investment in computers and the accessories, they must plan ahead, determine their goals, provide in-depth training, and offer support to computer users. In this way, all individuals involved with the student's performance will learn to benefit from technology.

Research on classroom computer application (Morgan, 1993; Vaughn et al., 1997) strongly suggests that technology for high-risk students provides motivation and skill development and has increased processing skills. The phrase *any child can learn* becomes an authentic development when educating high-risk children with the use of technology. Toward this end, this chapter first describes what computers can do for students and staff. Second, it reviews effective uses of technology in the classroom as well as how practical computer applications and Internet access can motivate skill development and enrich the scope and sequence of curriculum, instruction, and assessment for all children.

WHAT COMPUTERS CAN DO FOR STUDENTS AND STAFF

Research suggests that using computers in schools can increase staff and student productivity and enhance interest in learning for all students. These benefits can occur only if computers are integrated into everyday activities. The National Association of Elementary School Principals (NAESP) adopted the belief that computers can affect education in the areas of (1) teacher and student productivity, (2) multimodal/multimedia instruction, (3) teacher support, (4) administrative functions, (5) telecommunications, and (6) adaptive uses.

Teacher and Student Productivity

Both teachers and students can become more productive as they learn to use computers for old and new tasks. Word processing, database, and spreadsheet programs are just a few of the applications that can save time and offer motivation to all students, especially students who are high-risk and have special needs.

Word Processing

Learning word processing skills can help teachers with many duties, such as writing letters to parents and creating tests. While features such as spell check and grammar check are controversial when it comes to student use, there is no doubt that revising work is easier for students with "copy," "delete," and "paste" features. Also, easy access to an on-line dictionary or thesaurus can encourage high-risk children to use these references, creating a better-quality writing task.

More and more teachers are using word processors to plan their lessons. With word processors, teachers can easily copy a lesson plan framework (including spaces for lesson objectives, materials, assignments, homework, assessment, and procedures), move information, and make frequent changes. For teachers who want to use more sophisticated systems, Vaughn et al. (1997) recommend computer software specifically designed for instructional planning. For example, *Bradford Lesson Planner and Bradford Class Manager* (William K. Bradford Publishing Company, 1-800-421-2009) are Windows Programs for developing and printing lesson plans and student data. *The Bradford Lesson Planner* includes formatted lesson plans with spaces for lesson objectives, textbook information, supplemental materials, and lesson notes. Similar in function is the weekly planner software by Macintosh called *Plan to Teach.* This helps teachers develop daily and weekly plans, as well as plans for individual students. It also provides guidelines for setting up beginning of the year classroom routines and seating charts.

Computer-assisted instruction (CAI) involves learning through the use of computers and multimedia systems. In contrast, computer-managed assessment and instruction involves computers and multimedia systems to obtain and manage information about the learner and learning resources. Student-directed research on word processing (Bangert-Drowns, 1993; Cochran-Smith, 1991; Higgins & Boone, 1993) indicates that text programs combined with writing instruction consistently produce a positive, albeit small, impact on students' writing and their attitude toward writing. Failures usually have nothing to do with the software per se. Software provides only a *learning tool*, not the *learning process.* Additionally required in word processing for students with special needs is *systematic instruction* in writing.

Using microcomputers for word processing holds great promise not only for students with writing challenges but also for students who have problems composing or spelling or with fine and gross motor difficulties. Using word processing software, students can revise and edit text more easily and can publish a neat, legible final product. Majsterek (1990), for example, made the following initial recommendations about using microcomputers:

1. Select computer software that emphasizes a process approach to writing (i.e., prewriting, composing, revising, editing, publishing). Examples are *The Ultimate Writing and Creativity Center and Student Writing and Research* Center (The Learning Company, 1-800-852-2255), *The Writing Workshop* (Milliken Publishing, 1-800-643-0008), and *Kidsworks,* (Davidson & Associates, 1-800-545-7677).

2. Make certain that students are familiar with the writing process before you introduce them to computer software.

3. Review the software manual and either adapt it for students with reading problems or develop cue sheets to simplify procedures.

4. Bear in mind that, for many students, concurrently learning keyboarding, machine skills, and writing software commands can be a demanding task. Teach basic keyboarding and machine skills before you introduce writing process software.

5. Keep a balance between writing with and without a word processor so that students will work on handwriting, spelling, and composition skills in both modes.

Databases

Databases store, retrieve, and organize information, which allows students to ask computers questions about certain topics. For example, students might ask a database to separately list dinosaurs that lived in water and those that lived on land or which dinosaurs were meat eaters as opposed to plant eaters.

Spreadsheets

Spreadsheet programs can be used to keep track of patterns, numbers, or other quantitative information. For example, as students test hypotheses and study causal relationships using databases, they can track their findings by using spreadsheet programs. Such programs not only provide a visual image of findings but also check and summarize data in an organized form. Teachers and children can track behaviors, using daily points and graphs, to see if there is a pattern in specific target behaviors. Teachers can also use spreadsheets to keep track of grades or attendance.

Multimodal/Multimedia Instruction

In the past, teachers probably employed several types of equipment to create a multimedia presentation. Today, teachers and students can design and create multimedia programs of their own using less equipment to achieve faster results. Interactive multimedia found on a CD-ROM or videodisc provides different kinds of information that can be accessed in any order through *hypermedia*. Hypermedia refers to links in a program that connect the hyperlearner random access to the contents by clicking on words or images. CD-ROMs can provide an incredible amount of text, graphics, audio, and video on a variety of subjects. Some even provide complete lesson plans. Other multimedia applications, such as desktop publishing programs, can allow teacher and students to create newsletters, books, and other professional-looking documents.

Authoring tools such as *HyperCard*, *The Digital Chisel*, and *PowerPoint* permit teachers to create their own interactive multimedia lessons. As an alternative to starting from scratch, teachers can also select, reorder, and customize components from databases called tool kits. Vaughn et al. (1997) found that the *Bio-Sci II Video Tool Kit* from Video Discovery (1-800-548-3472), for example, is a large database of images, film clips, and textual data on the natural sciences. Teachers can use key words to locate specific topics and resources. They then select, resequence, and add their own material to incorporate their selections into a lesson. Software manufacturers offer many services for adaptive software users. For example, Pierian Spring Software (1-800-472-8578), which publishes the *Digital Chisel*, offers a monthly subscription to educational clip media that teachers can integrate into multimedia lessons.

Teacher Support

Software-support resources supplement the teacher's instructional understanding of multimedia applications. However, instructors who are new to computers may be unaware of ways to access support-system resources. Novelli (1994) suggests six ways for teachers to make the most of technology:

1. *Request manuals.* After you compete a computer training program, request manuals for the equipment and programs you will be using. They can come in handy when problems or questions arise.

2. *Listen to students.* Ask them to tell you what they would like to do with technology and then work together to implement their suggestions.

3. *Connect a computer to a television.* Inexpensive devices that link computers to televisions are available through computer stores or catalogs. Using a television during large group computer activities can increase student interest.

4. *Use compatible programs.* If you own a computer, consider using the same programs at school and at home. This will allow you to carry disks back and forth instead of piles of paper.

5. *Collaborate.* Talk with other teachers about how they are using computers and software in the classroom. Brainstorm together about how technology can enhance lesson plans and integrate subjects and themes within the curriculum.

6. *Send home a newsletter.* Desktop publishing can make it easy and fun to produce a professional-looking class or school newsletter. Children love seeing their writing in print and sharing class news with parents.

Computer-launched training programs not only help with instruction but aid in constructing tests and logging student records. The following five applications particularly were found effective with high-risk and special needs students: *tuto-*

rial, drill and practice, simulation, testing, record keeping, and *homework help on the Internet.*

Tutorial

Tutorials are designed to present new information and introduce new skills and concepts. With the help of computers, tailoring instruction to individual students' needs has become easier. Tutorial programs, such as interactive videodisc programs, adjust and adapt lessons in response to students' answers and work. Programs can even help students work toward target goals with academics and behavior.

Kelly et al. (1987), for example, compared interactive videodisc programs with traditional basal mathematics programs for teaching fractions to students. They found that the interactive video programs outscored basal programs on both the posttest and the maintenance checks. The researchers ascribed the success of interactive videodiscs to the following attributes:

1. They systematically reviewed previously taught skills.
2. There were discrimination practices among the different strategies.
3. Numerous examples were provided.
4. The terms "numerator" and "denominator" were taught separately.
5. The programs explicitly taught different strategies for problem solving.

Interactive computer applications also help students visualize information, which fosters problem solving. Students with learning deficits can also perform mathematical word-problem solving on the computer. Students made substantial gains and reported that the pictorial information helped them with word problems.

Drill and Practice

Drill and practice skills reinforce skills previously taught, provide practice opportunities on skills and concepts, and provide feedback regarding progress. However, on the downside, critics fault this computer application as an expensive way to provide students with flash cards. Drill and practice programs have improved over time. When used judiciously, modern programs can help children learn and save teachers' time.

Simulation

Simulation presents decision making and cause-and-effect situations and de- emphasizes right or wrong answers. Simulation programs allow students to apply classroom lessons to real-life situations. For example, a program that simulates flying (e.g., *Flight Simulator*) can teach about altitude and many other aviation concepts.

Testing

While regular tests can be administered on computers, so can frequent measurements of students' skill levels. Some testing programs not only assess a student's individual progress but also make recommendations for further learning or remediation due to patterns on past work that has been saved and analyzed in the database.

Record Keeping

Computers can help teachers and students organize and store everything from individual student portfolios to seating charts and grades. If the school's computers are networked, records can be shared among teachers, administrators, and support personnel.

Homework Help on the Internet

Students may have many questions that arise after classroom hours. Students should have help available during evening hours, when most are doing their homework. According to Rivard (1997), the Internet has dozens of bulletin boards, chat rooms, and other forums that give students the opportunity to ask for help with most school-related homework problems. A variety of these services have certified teachers on-line to answer student homework questions. Commercial service providers recruit teachers to become on-line electronic tutors. Many times, teachers are usually reimbursed for their time with free on-line time with the service provider. On-line tutors will work through your students' questions, offering tips and explanations, not just doling out answers. The following places are suggestions where homework help may be found:

1. America On-Line (AOL): Academic Assistance Center. Search word—*Homework*. Live chat with real teachers between 5:00 P.M. and 1:00 A.M., every day (EST). In addition to this service, AOL provides a teacher paging service. Search word—*teacher pager*. Type in your grade level, your questions, and click/send. E-mail answers are guaranteed within 48 hours.

2. Any Internet Source: Teacher paging on the Internet. Enter this address: homework24@aol.com.

3. CompuServe: See the Student's Forum search word—*go stufo*.

4. Genie: Access the Computer Assisted Learning Center. Homework questions are posted by subject. Real-time chat is available Mondays and Wednesdays, 9:00 P.M.–10:00 P.M. (EST) and Tuesdays and Thursdays, 10:00 P.M.–11:00 P.M. (EST).

5. Prodigy: Access the Education Bulletin Board or Homework Helper. Helper is a premium service, and an extra charge is assigned for services rendered.

Administrative Functions

Administrators' computers are most helpful when they are part of a schoolwide network. Being connected to others' computers can provide quick access to student information and other shared resources. For example, a network might give an administrator immediate access to student grades in individual classes or to records for exceptional children with an individual education plan (IEP). That way, teachers instantly know the special students' accommodation plan under Section

504 in accordance with Public Law 93-112. Other clear advantages of schoolwide computer networks among staff are *e-mail,* *Web sites,* and *bulletin board services.*

E-mail

E-mail is an electron mail that allows you to have an address on the information highway. Another important benefit of networking is the ability to send internal e-mail instead of wasting time and supplies printing and distributing memos. E-mail permits administrators and others to send multiple messages in a matter of seconds. Teachers can send or receive messages to any number of the Internet users around the world. A CompuServe user can just as easily communicate with a university mainframe user, a direct connect user, a BBS user, or an America On-Line (AOL) user.

Web Sites

Visiting the Web gives users a break from text-only Net surfing. Teachers can experience refreshing multimedia-based information gleaned from Web sites that contain pictures, graphics, animation, and sound or video information. For example, at *http://www.abduct. com,* users discover a kaleidoscope of high-tech, glossy pictures and sample video and audio files and bulletin board discussion regarding mysteries of alien abduction phenomena. Many listed or pictured resources may be in public domain or permit downloading into .TIF or .TXT files for later review and dissemination for instructional purposes only.

Bulletin Board Services (BBS)

Accessing the bulletin board services (BBS) entitles you to all of the information posted on the selection of the BBS. Live chat lines might be established for academic purposes, entertainment purposes, or social purposes. The only downfall of BBS is overuse. Users intrigued by lively exchange in chat rooms may become addicted to seeing how people respond to their posted ideas and awaiting discussion with reliable peer users. Overuse may not only interfere with teacher–student instructional time but also result in computer abuse. This is where teachers habitually using Internet access exclusively for chat rooms or for cultivating peer and even romantic contacts lose sight of the computer's educational value. Strangely, computer abuse is on the rise and usually deserves noteworthy mention in administrative policies describing teacher-computer usage.

TELECOMMUNICATIONS

While a network makes it possible to communicate within your school, telecommunications allows interaction with the outside world. With the help of modems and special software, students and staff can access the Internet to gain information from a variety of sources and to communicate with other students. Of course, on-line ventures require careful planning and close supervision so that students do not have access to inappropriate materials.

Telecommunications can include using videography to create community videos. Creating videos of the home community integrates multicultural education and the student's home communities into the curriculum. This activity provides students the opportunity to learn about, and celebrate, their home communities and cultures while at the same time learning basic videography skills. Vaughn et al. (1997) stated that even as simple a process as having students video typical scenes around the community and interview respected members of the community has opportunities for planning the video, developing storyboards, and writing and conducting interviews. If editing equipment is available, students can learn simple editing skills by piecing together the segments of videotape as they construct the community video.

Constructing a community video provides many opportunities to learn about the community's people and interests. A community video can focus on one context or incorporate many different ones. For example, an upper elementary class might decide to focus on home life, traditions, and celebrations, whereas a high school American government class might select a political issue such as illegal immigrants for their community video. Constructing a community video provides an ideal opportunity for students to learn basic videography skills, such as setting up the camera, focusing and adjusting the zoom, framing the subjects, and learning to use external microphones for interviews. Students would also be responsible for writing the interview and practicing their interviewing skills with each other. They will integrate scenes from the arts with their interviews to make the video interesting and to provide pictures of what is being described.

Broome and White (1995) discuss the many uses of videotape in the classroom, especially those that serve high-risk students with behavioral disorders. The authors indicate that technology offers ways for teachers to deal effectively with students with behavioral challenges. Technological devices, including wrist counters, golf counters, grocery counters, index cards for tally marks, beads in pocket, and printing calculators can assist teachers in recording student behaviors. Twelve objectives, according to the authors, promote the use of videotaping to help manage students with emotional and behavioral challenges:

1. To provide a permanent antecedent-behavior-consequence (ABC) analysis.

2. To self-monitor one's behavioral strengths and weaknesses.

3. To evaluate peer behavioral strengths and weaknesses.

4. To provide reality replay on facial expressions, body language, expressions of feelings, tone of voice, and other hard-to-define performance criteria.

5. To provide motivation and enthusiasm for group sessions.

6. To add vitality to simulations and role playing.

7. To reinforce shared experience.

8. To catch unobserved misbehavior or adaptive behaviors.

9. To provide a less intrusive consequence for misbehavior.

10. To give parents and other agencies a realistic perspective on child misbehavior and classroom interventions.

11. To build cooperation and trust.

12. To plan for inclusion with special education students.

Both students and teachers can benefit from being involved in a cutting-edge, creative process. These programs can offer teachers unique development and effective teaching materials and help students to create interactive, multimedia presentations. Jointly working on projects can boost student motivation and support active learning through an interdisciplinary process.

Collaboration and Computers

Through the use of computer software, teachers can collaborate with school personnel in other cities and states and even different countries. Synchronous collaboration occurs when the individuals involved interact at the same time (Collis & Heeren, 1993). *Aspects* is an example of a computer program that enables the user to engage in synchronous collaboration. This computer program allows its users to open and work on the same file(s). Changes made to the file by one user will appear on the screens of all of the current participants. In this manner, users can work together, simultaneously changing text files and drawing files of a shared document. *Aspects* is available from Group Logic (1-800-476-8781).

A synchronous collaboration occurs when the participants communicate with each other not only from different places but also at different times. For example, *Common Knowledge* allows its users to modify a shared document at any time. Each user then has access to the most recent version of the document, as well as its original version. Commands within the program allow the user to view which specific changes have been made to the document, when these changes were made, and by whom. *Common Knowledge* is available from On Technology (1-800-548-8871).

The importance and value of collaboration is vital in effective teaching. Technological advancements such as *Aspects* and *Common Knowledge* provide teachers with greater opportunities and increased flexibility in collaboration.

ADAPTIVE USES

Some of the most exciting advances in computing are those that can help students who are high-risk with special needs. For example, students with communication disorders can use speech synthesizers, which generate speech as users type in their words.

Audiotaping

Audiotaped books are increasingly popular and acceptable to students. Children can listen to the tapes in a listening center in elementary classrooms, resource rooms, or school media centers or at home. Audiotaping, along with the hard copy of the audiotape, is especially effective with high-risk children, children with attention deficits, and children exhibiting behavior challenges. Use of audiotaped books helps the children to focus, offering a multimodal approach to their independent tasks. Other helpful devices include those that convert text files into audio files so they can be heard by nonreaders or children who are visually challenged.

High-tech equipment has created an easier integration into the regular classroom for the student with low vision. For example, computer screen magnification systems make print available to students with low vision. Systems can have other features as well, such as braille displays and printers. *Braille 'n Speak* is a rechargeable computer, weighing less than a pound, that can serve as a word processor, stopwatch, calendar, and clock (Espinola, 1992). Other products are designed for people who are braille-literate, like *Power Braille and Braille Mate from TeleSensory* (1-415-960-0920). The keys correspond to those on a broiler. An individual who is visually challenged can braille on the *Braille 'n Speak* and, with the speech synthesizer, can hear the material that has been Brailled in, a letter, word, sentence, paragraph, or entire file at a time. Information can be transferred by connecting the device to an external braille printer, standard printer, modem, or another computer.

According to Smith et al. (1998), there are technology-based applications that can effectively assist students with their individual areas of need. For example, if the student has deficits in basic academic subjects and skills, the drill and practice software, integrated learning systems, and hypermedia technology have proven effective with all ability levels. Another suggestion for students with short attention spans is utilization of videodiscs. All technology-based application, especially computer games and programs, will help students with motivational challenges.

Computer games can be used to promote motivation as well as the social acceptance and peer interaction of students with special needs (Lewis, 1993). *Interaction Games, Interaction Games II,* and *Games 2 Play for Apple II* (Don Johnston Developmental Equipment, Inc., 1-800-999-4660) provide opportunities for students to engage in both competitive and cooperative games. The cooperative games require that each student manipulate an independent switch, but only through the combined efforts of both students can the game be won. Such interactions can foster the idea that students with behavior problems have strengths and abilities that are beneficial to others in the class and can provide a context for students to relate with their classmates. Teachers can manipulate the competitive games so that students of different ability levels can compete for more equal starting positions. Similar products exist for Windows and Macintosh platforms, including curriculum-related applications, such as cooperative storytelling and math problem-solving games.

High-Tech Alternatives for Talented and Gifted Learners

According to Trotter (1991), children who are gifted and talented need access to contemporary tools that bring incredible amounts of information to their fingertips in an instant. Urban children from high-risk backgrounds often fall into the talented and gifted category, thriving on challenging curriculum. Emerging technologies include personal computers, CD-ROM, supercomputers, laser disc players, and telecommunications networks. Interactive videodiscs, such as *The National Gallery of Art* (Voyager Company, 1-800-446-2001), can bring the world of art to students. Access to on-line services such as AOL (1-800-227-6364) and Prodigy (1-800-284-5933) can help students retrieve information and communicate with others through the Internet.

Dale (1993) describes technology that allows students with multiple intelligences and academic talents to increase their productivity by using CD-ROMS for literature searches and developing multimedia presentations for school. Other computer applications suggestions were Programming (e.g., BASIC, LOGO, Pascal), Computer Assisted Instruction (CAI), word processing, databases, spreadsheets, and telecommunications.

In that same vein, Morgan (1993) stated that Computer Assisted Design (CAD) and other art activities (e.g., using color graphics with the Amiga System), as well as music synthesis and music instrument digital interface (MIDI), would allow learners to take an active role in their education. Students who are talented and gifted should have access to technology to facilitate their instructional needs. Numerous programs are appropriate for students who display multiple intelligences or talents or are certified gifted in specific areas, encouraging them to think of their own ways of using the computer to gather and analyze information. By using new technologies, all learners can take an active role in their education, stretching beyond the walls of the classroom.

EFFECTIVE USE OF TECHNOLOGY IN THE CLASSROOMS

There seems to be some concern as to how to effectively use computers in the classroom. This section focuses on elementary students, grades kindergarten through fifth, largely because computer *basics must be established in the early grades.* Using technology as an integrated part of each lesson changes the way students think and learn for the rest of their lives. Curricular standards and objectives are suggested, along with ideas for practical computer station programming.

Computer Skill Objectives

The following is a sequential series of objectives for computer training at different grade levels adapted from North Carolina Computer Standards. Each criterion-based curriculum teaches prerequisite skills enabling rapid progression from one step to successive steps. Student learning thereby is cumulative. Acquired skills in earlier grades assure a knowledge base for more complex computer usage by the time students reach middle and high school levels.

Kindergarten

1. Identify the physical components of a computer system (monitor, keyboard, disk drive, printer).

2. On a keyboard, identify letters, numbers, and other commonly used keys (return, enter, space bar).

3. Use the computer as a machine that helps students learn.

4. Demonstrate correct use of a computer (follow the computer care rules posed in each classroom).

First Grade

1. Identify the physical components of a computer system (monitor, keyboard, disk drive, printer).

2. On a keyboard, identify letters, numbers, and other commonly used keys (return, enter, space bar, shift key, delete/backspace, arrow keys).

3. Identify fundamental computer terms (disk, software, hardware, booting/starting, cursor).

4. Demonstrate correct use of a computer (follow the computer care rules posted in each classroom).

5. Demonstrate correct use of hardware and software.

Second Grade

1. Identify the physical components of a computer system (monitor, keyboard, disk drive, CPU [central processing unit], printer)

2. Locate and use symbol keys and special function keys (period, question mark, caps lock, arrow keys, shift).

3. Identify word processing terms (word processing, cursor, load, save, print).

4. Demonstrate correct keyboarding posture and finger placement for the entire row keys.

5. Demonstrate beginning word processing techniques including saving, printing, and retrieving text.

6. Demonstrate correct use of hardware and software.

Third Grade

1. Identify the physical components of a computer system as either input, output, or processing devices.

2. Demonstrate proper keyboarding techniques.

3. Identify word processing terms (word processing, cursor, lead, save, and print).

4. Use *The Writing Center* to load, enter, save, print, and retrieve text.

5. Demonstrate correct use of hardware and software.

6. Use commercial software in content areas.

7. Identify computers as tools for accessing information.

Fourth Grade

1. Demonstrate proper keyboarding techniques.

2. Identify word processing terms (word processing, cursor, load, save, and print).

3. Use *MicroSoft Works* to enter, save, print, and retrieve text.

4. Use *MicroSoft Works* to edit a paragraph and save changes.

5. Describe the difference between a print database and a computer database.

6. Demonstrate correct use of hardware and software.

7. Use commercial software in content areas.

8. Identify computers as tools for accessing information.

Fifth Grade

1. Demonstrate proper keyboarding techniques.

2. Use *MicroSoft Works* to enter, save, print, and retrieve text.

3. Use *MicroSoft Works* to copy and move text.

4. Use *MicroSoft Works* to publish a report that contains centering, tabs, and more than one paragraph.

5. Identify database management terms (database, file, record, field/category, sort/arrange, select/search, report).

6. Use a prepared database to enter and edit data.

7. Identify telecomputing terms (modem, upload, download, bulletin board, E-mail).

8. Use commercial software in content areas.

9. Use telecomputing hardware and software to communicate with a distant computer or an on-line service.

Practical Station Suggestions for Using Technology in the Classroom

Using technology in the classroom is most effective when positioned as a learning center or *station*. The teacher can rotate students through the stations or the students can use them based on *who is ready* or *individual needs*. "Who is ready" refers to students who have copiloted a final draft of their writing and are ready to type it using the word processing program. "Based on individual needs" refers to students that either need to be challenged or may need remediation, for example, a fifth grader working on algebra by using the program *Algeblaster*, or the first grader who still does not recognize letters and needs to work on *A to Zap* or *Muppets on Stage* programs. In some cases, the teacher will want to develop activities around the software. The only difference is that the teacher is utilizing the computer as the learning tool.

Computer stations identifiable from other classroom stations also mark the area for students to apply software programs. As students discover the station, ultimately using it independently, self-teaching increases as a viable learning mechanism. Self-teaching results, however, only when available software and station rules facilitate self-guided instruction. For example, never log-in for students. Self-initiated logging helps students get acquainted with the machine and properly proceed through a chain of icon-clicking key strokes. Similar software and instructional guidelines are offered here according to grade level.

Practical Station Suggestions for Kindergarten and First Grade

1. Letter Recognition: *Muppets on Stage, A to Zap.*

2. Numbers/Early Math Concepts: *Muppets on Stage, Muppet Math, KidsMath.*

3. Addition/Subtraction: *MathBlaster, Rocket Launcher.*

4. Writing: *The Writing Center* (lots of pictures to use in writing). Refer to *The Writing Center* timeline (next section) to teach the appropriate word processing skills at the appropriate grade level.

5. Reading: *Reader Rabbit 1, Reader Rabbit 2, Accelerated Reader.*

6. Reading (above grade level): *Reading Magic Library* (favorites are "Jack and the Beanstalk" or "Flodd the Bad Guy"). The students can read, record, or rewrite the story. Good for making predictions. Must read at second- or third-grade level.

7. Graphing: *The Graph Club* (makes graphs and prints them).

8. Science: *Learn About, More Learn About* (plants, animals, dinosaurs, the night sky, etc.), *The Living Books.*

Practical Station Suggestions for Second and Third Grade

1. Writing: *The Writing Center* (type poems, stories, reports, etc.). Refer to *The Writing Center* timeline to teach the appropriate word processing skills at your grade level.

2. Reading (grade level or below): *Reader Rabbit 2* (compound words, a, b, c order)

3. Reading (above grade level): *Reading Magic Library* ("Jack and the Beanstalk" or "Flodd the Bad Guy"). Good for making predictions and rewriting the stories.

4. Math (functional grade level): *MathBlaster* (addition, subtraction, multiplication, division), *Rocket Launcher.* Make sure students are not in the menu STUDY, or it will give them the answers.

5. Math (above grade level): *Math Problem Solvers* (levels 3–6), all areas of math.

6. *World Book Encyclopedia,* Volume D: Type WB when you log in. Allows brighter and more independent students to do research on selected topics.

7. Graphing: *The Graph Club* (makes graphs and prints them).

8. *EasyBook*: Students can write their own books.

9. Develop activities around software such as *New Kid on the Block* (CDs) that focus on poetry.

Practical Station Suggestions for Fourth and Fifth Grade

1. Writing: *Microsoft Works* (word processing).

2. Research: Internet (research various topics), *World Book.*

3. Math: *MathBlaster* (subtraction, multiplication, division, fractions; proper, improper, mixed numbers, percents, decimals). Stay in Rocket Launcher for drill. Make sure students are not in the STUDY menu, as that gives them the answers.

4. Math (above grade level): *Math Problem Solvers, AlgeBlaster*

5. Social Studies/Geography: *Carmen World* (critical reading, taking notes, geography), *National Inspirer* (U.S. geography), *Dig It!*

6. Science: *InnerBody Works* (human body).

Improving Computer Equity

One of the realities of computers is that they are expensive. A home computer is simply not in the budget for many students from low-income families. Many schools in low-income areas, where additional money for computers (often donated by parent organizations) is not available, have fewer computers than schools in high-income areas. Maddux et al. (1992) suggests that for schools with large numbers of at-risk students, computers are likely to be used for drill in basic skills, whereas in wealthier schools, computers are more likely to be used to teach programming. In the future, students without basic computer skills suffer a tremendous disadvantage in terms of employability. Therefore, issues of computer equity-equal access to computers in the school are a current and serious concern.

Dale (1993) offers the following suggestions to initiate improvement toward computer equity:

1. Structure opportunities for computer access before and after school. Consider starting a computer club.
2. Include instruction in word processing, database management, spreadsheet usage, and computer programming.
3. Include instructional opportunities to use software to improve basic skills.
4. Select software that encourages problem solving and higher-order thinking.
5. Select software that helps make connections between basic skills and real-life situations.

PLANNING FOR TECHNOLOGICAL INTEGRATION

The first step in preparing for new technology is to decide who will actually do the planning. Whether it will be done on the school or district level, a special planning team should be formed to focus on short-term and long-term goals. While it might seem logical to appoint computer-literate staff members to the team, it is best to choose all types of participants so that the committee truly represents your diverse staff. However, a technology coordinator may be needed to help the committee understand current technology trends. With this in mind, there are a few basic questions that need to be answered before considering any technological purchases.

1. How can technology enhance our students' education? It is important to be clear about what the technology does for students. Consider visiting other schools where computers are being used successfully.
2. How will new technology affect current educational practices? If new technology serves its purpose, it will change the way students at each school learn. The changes will need support from administrators and teachers. Our future educators will ultimately be responsible for implementing the new technological approaches.

3. Which software will produce the results you desire? After deciding what the school needs, choose software that accomplishes the goals and objectives of teacher curricula. Select software *before* choosing computer hardware.

4. Will you network? Deciding whether to link computers to each other is a complicated issue, and it is recommended to consult with a computer specialist. Although networking is a big step, the rewards are often worth the effort.

5. Where will computers be located? Although there may still be a role for the centralized computer lab, trends are to place computers in the classroom. Placing computers in a lab or media center makes them more difficult to integrate into the regular class routines.

6. Do you have to train the staff? Yes. Train all staff. Do not invest in new technology unless there will be adequate and ongoing training for the entire staff.

COMMON MISTAKES TO AVOID

According to Wilson (1996), buying computers and peripherals can be confusing. Budget-minded administrators can be persuaded by vendors who are convincing about the newest, most expensive equipment on the market. The following suggestions of what *not to do* may help the school avoid some potential purchasing pitfalls:

1. *Buying bottom-of-the-line products.* Saving money is important, but computers near the low end in price may be a poor investment. In the past, for example, some schools saved money by buying computers without hard disk drives. Now these computers are obsolete, while hard disk drives are the standard. In other words, spending a little more now may save a lot of money in the long run.

2. *Buying cutting-edge products.* On the other hand, investing in extremely avant-garde technology may go beyond computer user literacy. Experts suggest that schools give new technology about a year to be tested and improved or rejected before considering a purchase. Sometimes, however, companies offer schools the opportunity to test new products. Consider taking advantage of such offers on a small scale.

3. *Focusing on the present.* Technology is improving so quickly that sometimes it seems that no matter what one buys, it will become obsolete almost immediately. That is why it is so important to design technology systems with the future in mind. Avoid choosing a system designed to help achieve only one goal, such as raising math scores. Instead, choose a system that is flexible and has room for expansion.

4. *Repairing old machines.* Upgrading old computers is fine, but there comes a time when it is worth it to spend money on new technology. Not only can investing in old machines become a waste of funds, but it can also keep students from learning about important new technologies.

5. *Using old software on new computers.* There is no reason to buy new computers if one is simply going to run old software on them. Invest in new computers only if the plan is to use updated or new software.

6. *Staff training.* Research and expert opinion suggest that *staff training is the key to the success of technology use.* It is often neglected by schools and school districts.

Wilson (1996) also suggests the following materials, which can be purchased from Educational Research Service (ERS), an independent, nonprofit research foundation. ERS is sponsored by seven national school management associations to serve as the research and information source for local school and school district decisions. To order materials from ERS, contact: Educational Research Service, Publication Orders, 2000 Clarendon Blvd., Arlington, VA 22201. Phone: 1-800-791-9308; fax: 1-800-791-9309.

1. *The Internet Roadmap for Educators.* This 91-page book provides both an overview of issues related to educational use of the Internet and a concrete, easy-to-use guide to enhancing learning through the Internet. Base price: $20.

2. *The Guide to the Internet for Parents.* This brochure is designed to answer some of parents' most common questions about children's accessing the Internet from school or home. The *Guide* is provided as an 8½ x 11-inch, two-page original, which is ready to reproduce in as many copies as needed within your school and folds into a six-panel brochure. Base price: $26.

Researchers (Dale, 1993; Morgan, 1993; Trotter, 1991; Wilson, 1996) highly recommend the following resources for teachers and administrators on the Internet:

1. *Teacher's Edition On-Line.* This resource contains a wide variety of teaching tips and lesson plans. Visitors can pose a question or leave a tip for other educators. *http://www.ncrel.org/ncrel.*

2. *Pathways to School Improvement.* This resource offers descriptions of successful improvement efforts, collections of materials to support change, and research. *http://www.ncrel.org/ncrel.*

3. *Busy Teacher's Web Site.* This resource serves as a one-stop Internet location for busy teachers, grouping classroom Internet resources by subject area. *http//www.ceismc.gatech.edu/BusyT.*

4. *AskERIC Virtual Library.* This resource contains lesson plans, links to the Discovery Channel, a collection of professional education articles, and more. *http://ericir.syr.edu* or *gopher://ericir/syr.edu.*

5. *Teaching and Learning Search.* This resource contains searchable collections of more than 450 sites related to educational and academic topics. *http://www.mcli.dist.maricopa,edu/tl/.*

6. *Ligature Home Page.* This resource contains designs and sells core curriculum over the Internet. *http://academy3.ligature.com.*

5

CULTURAL DIVERSITY
IN THE CLASSROOM

Nancy R. Macciomei

Children who are at risk are differentiated by their difficulty or inability to meet the standards for school success. As more children are identified as at risk, especially in our urban areas, teacher education programs must become responsive in training future teachers to work with children from diverse backgrounds. Demographic research has demonstrated that a disproportionate number of at-risk children come from lower socioeconomic status homes or homes where English is not the native language. This background is in contrast to the bulk of America's teachers, who come from middle-class, English-speaking settings (McGrew-Zoubi & Brown, 1995). Teachers not only have the challenge of educating all children within the regular classroom but they also grapple with the question of how to respond to diverse learning needs and abilities among those children.

Diversity has many facets: cultural, religious, linguistic, ethnic, racial, mental and physical abilities, social, economic, age, and gender. This chapter responds to what Turnbull et al. (1995) regard as cultural diversity. It refers to the many different factors that shape one's sense of group identity, including race, geographical locations, gender, and occupations. Cultures are dynamic, complex, and changing. It is the *way of life* of a social group to adapt to the environment and modify the setting in which they live. Even though an outsider can learn to speak the various languages of other social groups, this accomplishment does not allow complete access to understanding the group's mores and customs. People who share a particular culture's ideas and values usually interpret events in similar ways. Although membership in a specific cultural group does not determine behavior, members are exposed to the same set of expectations and consequences for acting in certain ways. Banks (1994b) states that certain types of behavior become more probable within similar cultures. It is also important to remember that each student is a member of multiple groups according to race, ethnicity, social class, religion, gender, and disability. Each of these groups exerts various degrees of influence on the student's ways of interpreting and responding to the world.

During the last few decades, educators have experimented with a variety of alternative innovations to enrich the culturally diverse, including students' academic, social, and emotional growth, especially within urban areas. These innovations included mainstreaming, inclusion, and detracking. The intent was to reach out to all students. Although the intent was there, most strategies and outcomes were not successful. To add to the challenge of responding to a diversity of learning needs, educators are simultaneously being asked to raise standards for their students. To successfully reach out to a diversity of learners requires substantial support. According to Kerr and Nelson (1998), educators who receive substantial help are more effective when carrying out worthwhile innovations that increase all students' potential for success.

This notion of support is vitally important because the culturally diverse, at-risk population is growing throughout the nation. Administrators and educators must begin to take an active role in alternative programming, providing for all students, and continuing to believe in the efficacy of raising academic standards for all children. Consequently, this chapter provides information on common concerns and issues with multicultural teaching, effective communication toward motivating all learners, and suggested instructional activities and resources for teachers.

COMMON CONCERNS AND ISSUES WITH MULTICULTURAL TEACHING

Gollnick and Chinn (1994) outline four basic characteristics of culture that provide a background for considering the concerns, issues, and special needs of culturally diverse students and their families.

1. *Our cultural heritage is learned.* It is not innately based on the culture in which we are born. Middle Eastern infants adopted by Italian American, Catholic, middle-class parents share a cultural heritage with middle-class, Italian American Catholics, rather than Middle Eastern, Iraqi culture.

2. *Culture is shared.* Shared cultural patterns and customs bind people together in an identifiable group and make it possible for them to live together and function with ease. Groups may not realize the common cultural aspects as existent in the cultural group, that is, the way they communicate with each other and the foods they eat.

3. *Culture is an adaptation.* Cultures have developed to accommodate certain environmental conditions and available natural and technological resources. For example, Eskimo who live with extreme cold, snow, ice, seals, and the sea have developed a culture different from that of the Pacific Islander. The culture of urban residents differs from that of rural residents, in part, because of the resources available in the different settings.

4. *Culture is a dynamic system that changes continuously.* For example, the replacement of industrial workers by robots is changing the culture of many working-class communities in areas such as Detroit or Flint, Michigan.

Glenn (1989) states that we need an approach to education that takes seriously the ongoing culture of children and their families, not the folklore that had meaning for their grandparents. Unfortunately, some children from cultural backgrounds that are different from white, middle-class America still encounter institutionalized discrimination.

Discrimination that exists throughout our nation feeds into public schools. Educators are slowly realizing the benefits and necessity, as well as the ethical and moral correctness, of celebrating diversity. The evidence of this realization is the increasing emphasis on multicultural education.

According to Turnbull et al. (1995), multicultural education attempts to teach all children in ways that recognize the contributions of many cultures in the United States. Ball and Harry (1993) stated that multicultural education includes attention to staffing, environment, assessment, and curricula; their approach calls for reorganization that reflects the perspectives, of and knowledge about, diverse racial and ethnic groups. Also, a multicultural approach recognizes that families are diverse and requires adjustments in educational curricula. In this respect, Banks (1994a) identifies five major goals of multicultural approaches to education:

1. *To help individuals gain a greater self-understanding by viewing themselves from the perspectives of other cultures.* Students who are taught to understand and value their own culture and to acquaint themselves with other cultures gain an understanding and respect for other cultures.

2. *To provide students with cultural and ethnic alternatives.* Schools should move away from the traditional curriculum and teach students about the richness of music, literature, values, lifestyles, and perspectives that exist among other ethnic groups.

3. *To provide students with the skills, attitudes, and knowledge they need to function within their ethnic culture and the mainstream culture.* Multicultural education prepares students to function successfully in their home and ethnic communities, as well as in mainstream United States.

4. *To reduce the pain and discrimination that members of some ethnic and racial groups experience in schools and in the broader society.* Multicultural education provides ways to reduce prejudice and alienation of ethnically diverse students in school by empowering them and respecting their ethnic identity. Innovative clubs such as Minority Achievement Programs help celebrate the unique facets of each ethnic group, sharing foods, clothing, myths, geography, and so on, with the club, classrooms, and the entire school.

5. *To help students master essential literacy, numeracy, thinking, and perspective-taking skills.* Multicultural education assumes that students will master important skills if multiethnic and relevant content is integrated throughout the curriculum. Curricula must integrate units on foods, clothing, stories, legends, dances, and arts of the major American ethnic groups within an ongoing, daily curriculum. Advocates such as Grossman (1995) believe that the major goal of multicultural education is to transform the school so that students from diverse cultural, social-class, racial, and ethnic groups experience an equal opportunity to learn in school.

According to Banks (1994a), teachers should increase their understanding of current issues and appreciation of different ethnic and cultural groups by studying the following concepts:

- Origins and immigration
- Shared culture, values, and symbols
- Ethnic identity and sense of peoplehood
- Perspectives, worldview, and frames of reference
- Ethnic institutions and self-determination
- Demographic, social, political, and economic status
- Prejudice, discrimination, and racism
- Intraethnic diversity
- Assimilation and acculturation
- Revolution issues
- Knowledge construction
- Verbal and nonverbal communication styles of ethic groups

Teacher education programs should help in-service teachers to understand the issues and challenges involved with teaching the culturally diverse students who are represented in large urban areas across the nation. Effective teachers must develop not only cultural sensitivity but also knowledge and skills for implementing a culturally responsive curriculum. Also, a large part of working with students in schools is establishing school–family partnerships.

School–Family Involvement

Family involvement becomes an important component to becoming culturally competent. Reynolds (1992) reported on the positive influence of parental involvement on children's academic achievement and school adjustment. He discussed a strong relationship between parental involvement in school and the at-risk, urban child's development of self-confidence, motivation, and sense of cohesiveness. Also, families of students who did not drop out and who succeeded in school participated in their children's school decisions, demonstrated a motivating and nonpunitive action concerning grades, and were involved to different degrees within the school environment.

The demands and challenges for administrators and educators can become frustrating when actively trying to involve families from diverse backgrounds. Thomas et al. (1995) supported the following six notions about families from diverse ethnic backgrounds:

1. *Many families may be potentially English-proficient or less well educated, come from low social-economic background, or be undocumented immigrants.* This means that we provide materials in both the native and English language and preferably com-

municate with the family directly through home visits or by telephone. Some parents are not able to read their native language and may depend on older offspring to translate materials for them.

2. *Educators must understand that although the parents may not have finished school or are unable to read, they are life-educated.* This means they know their child better than anyone else does.

3. *If families are suspected to be undocumented immigrants, it is natural for them to be fearful of interaction with anyone representing authority.* Building trust and cooperation from families, even if undocumented immigrants, is important.

4. *Families from culturally diverse backgrounds tend to be family-oriented.* Extended family members may play important roles in child raising and family decisions.

5. *It is important to know that the family may hold idiosyncratic ideologies and practices about areas such as discipline and education.* For example, certain cultures teach their children *not* to look at an adult when they are being reprimanded. Children look at the ground or their feet to show respect and humility.

6. *The educational system and school officials may be extremely intimidating to the family.* It is also true that many ethnic families hold the professional educator or administrator on a pedestal and think the professional is the expert, not questioning or commenting on their own wishes for their child's education. Acting selfishly is inherently violating social customs.

Not only do educators have a wide range of culturally diverse students, but Jones and Carr (1995) state that educators have additional issues confronting them in the classroom. Common issues consist of:

1. All students learn at a different rate.

2. All students demonstrate different spans of ability.

3. Students learn in different ways, requiring a variety of instructional modalities.

4. Students begin learning as poor readers and inexperienced writers; they must practice each step in the scope and sequence of instruction.

5. Students do not know how to listen. They must be taught to respect and appreciate the thoughts of others.

6. Students do not process information well. It is important to reteach many areas of the curriculum to help students maintain and master the information.

7. Students need practice time. Practice time must be part of the daily routine .

EFFECTIVE COMMUNICATION TOWARD MOTIVATING DIVERSE LEARNERS

Meeting the motivational needs of a melting-pot population is not an easy task. First, in terms of the appropriate classroom environment, educators need to create a learner-centered setting. This setting would provide an optimum learning environment that recognizes students' need for support, group interaction, and hands-on instruction. This forum provides discovery within an individual's space.

This strategy of instruction also creates a relatively anxiety-free learning experience and offers creative centers that can offer thematic units within integrated subject areas. According to Wood and Long (1994), the learner-centered setting aims toward a kinship or notion of *group reference* as well as enhancing self-concepts.

The actual physical setting is also different from the traditional room with desks in a row. The desks are arranged in circles or small groups. Many times there are not desks at all. Use of rectangle tables or "hubs" that seat four in a grouping are effective for motivating responses and developing effective communication skills. These groupings are important to allow students to have direct eye contact with each other and constant communication between group members. The teacher supervises and guides students through the discovery lessons and is viewed more as the learning facilitator.

Mickler and Chaper (1989) stated that there is a serious need to take a look at the methods of instruction for motivating diverse and high-risk students in our urban areas. The time has come for educators to give absolute priority to the business of teaching. Teachers must use a variety of instructional techniques to meet each student's needs. There need to be less emphasis on tests and written assignments and more emphasis on group discussion and group goal setting. The emphasis should be on periodic, small-grouping activities. While in small groups, the teachers should facilitate group structuring, ensuring that groups include males, females, and task-oriented and socially oriented learners. Small-group situations should also foster learning strength diversity, creating situations where the more able help the less able and also learn more by *teaching*. The teacher should also circulate around the room and from group to group, becoming temporarily part of the learning activity of each group.

In addition, small-group discussion allows for, and encourages nonvocal students to voice ideas and ask questions. From time to time, classroom teachers should provide activity periods where students work independently on projects specifically designed to meet particular learning needs. When appropriate, we should incorporate computers, movies, laser discs (e.g., *Windows on Science Program*), television, reading machines, and other technical learning equipment into our classrooms. Teachers must respect their students, their thoughts, their opinions, and their feelings. When teachers approach each individual with dignity and respect, they will receive both, opening the door to educate each student. According to Banks (1994b), the students are writers and growing individuals who have something to say. Our goal, as educators, must be to build successful inclusion of diverse learners in the same classroom.

Effective integration of high-risk, multiculturally diverse learners usually requires multiple teaching and learning approaches. The following six instructional strategies have been found useful in teaching diverse learners.

Cooperative Learning

Cooperative learning, when used appropriately, can increase positive social interaction and alter moderate behavior problems among students of diverse ability levels. This method also gives each child a chance to contribute to the group. The following are key elements of effective cooperative learning, identified by Robert Slavin (1990):

1. *Heterogeneous grouping:* Children with different skills and backgrounds, including special education students, can work together.

2. *Shared leadership:* Responsibilities are given to each member of the group. For example, in literacy grouping, one member might be the literary luminary. This member would be responsible to discuss the highlights or the best part of the book.

3. *Individual accountability:* Children are held responsible for their individual performance within the group that will lead to a group rating.

4. *Positive interdependence:* All students are expected to help and learn from other group members.

5. *Goals:* Team members work together toward accomplishing specific tasks. Maintenance of skills is a priority.

6. *Observation and intervention:* Teachers monitor progress, offer help, and teach social skills when needed.

7. *Self-reflection:* Groups reflect on individual performance as well as group performance as a whole.

Peer Tutors

Many research studies support the benefits of peer and cross-age tutoring in heterogeneous settings. Tutoring programs have resulted in improved social skills, better attendance, and higher achievement for both tutors and tutees. Studies warn that peer tutors need training, scheduling support, and follow-up. Also, tutoring should not be a substitute for individual teacher attention.

Learning Centers

Learning centers give students the opportunity to work on tasks that meet their personal learning styles and interests. Although activities at each learning center differ, separate stations help students reach a common goal. For example, a learning center may offer one student the chance to read part of the "I Have a Dream" speech, by Martin Luther King; another child may listen to an audio version of the speech, and another may use the computer to click into the Internet and bring up the speech within various research programs available for student use.

Computer Technology

Computer technology can help the teacher provide equal opportunities for success in diverse classrooms. Computers and other electronics can help children with learning challenges to write, solve problems, and collaborate more effectively with their peers.

Varied Assignments

Teachers can also vary student activities by allowing children to make choices about assignments in and out of class. For instance, students might be asked to pick their favorite novel. Another technique is to vary assignments and offer lessons that help students develop a sense of self-expression. One effective example is a method called *freestyle writing* (Macciomei, 1992). It is a three-phase expressive writing activity that helps students develop a sense of expression and supports the concept that students' thoughts are initially more important than accuracy in spelling and grammar.

This is particularly valuable for a diverse and high-risk population that may have delays in various aspects of written language. The primary purpose of the activity is to help students develop independent, expressive, written language with ease and confidence. The activity's three phases may be spread out across weeks or months, depending on the individual abilities of the students. A secondary purpose is to enhance self-image, which may increase motivation to remain on task, altering behavior problems during instruction. As students realize that their ideas are important and worthwhile, their ability to express themselves increases. Many times, this new awareness transfers to other subject areas as well as affecting self-control and choice behaviors. The freestyle activity is implemented in three distinct phases.

Phase I

Introduce freestyle writing as a new way of expressing individual thoughts by writing them down without concern for spelling, sentence structure, or syntax. Students should concentrate on getting their thoughts and feelings on paper. In elementary classrooms, the teacher should tell the students that words will start in their heads, make their way down their arms, and come out of their pens or pencils. As students of all ages write continuously, words begin to flow. The important idea for the students to remember is to keep words coming and never stop writing until the time is up.

The teacher sets the timer for two minutes (elementary) or five minutes (secondary) and tells the students to begin writing. Two rules given are (1) no cursing on paper and (2) continue writing until they are told to stop (or hear the timer). If some students cannot think of anything to say, they should write that down until something pops into their minds. After the first five minutes, have the students stop, reread their papers, and ask themselves the following questions:

1. Does my freestyle writing sound like me talking?

2. Does it say what I was thinking?

3. Does it say what I wanted to say?

4. Did I write for the whole five minutes?

If most or all of the answers were yes, the students are then ready to move on to Phase II.

Phase II

After the students become familiar with the process in Phase I, increase the writing time to 5 minutes or more (elementary) or 10 minutes or more (secondary). Tell the students to pick one thought and expand on it. Allow the students to express individual feelings, opinions, known facts, and personal knowledge.

Phase III

The last phase is based on suggested prompts from the teacher. Set the timer for 10 minutes or more and write a one-word prompt on the chalkboard or overhead projector. Prompts such as "school," "friends," or "family" should motivate students enough to write nonstop for the designated time period. Teachers should focus on expanding opinions and personal experiences that are appropriate to the given prompt.

Self-evaluation, using the questions suggested in Phase I, will help students evaluate their initial success. As students continue to write, the teacher can compare the mechanics and content of written expression performed later in the school year with those of writing earlier in the year. Freestyle writing is an excellent source for a students portfolio. Use of rubrics to evaluate the writing, as well as offering credit or pass/fail grades may be more acceptable, especially when paired with specific feedback that fits each student's ability level.

Since expression of ideas, verbal or written, may be difficult for high-risk, urban children, a different activity that may be fun and motivating is to write down their random thoughts. Freestyle writing can reduce the impulse of acting out by satisfying the need to express themselves using an alternative technique: writing down their thoughts without the fear of getting a low grade regardless of grammar or spelling. This activity is adaptable to a wide variety of student abilities and can be practiced beginning at second grade. Freestyle writing has been implemented with considerable success in regular as well as special classrooms, across subject areas in elementary and secondary schools.

Evaluation

When instructional techniques change, evaluation systems must also be modified. Although Chapter 3 is devoted to alternative assessments, the following suggestions are informal, alternative assessment methods for teachers who work with diverse students in the classroom.

1. *Individualized tests.* It may take extra work, but personalized exams, oral or written, can help teachers better assess student progress in diverse classes. Modifying or adapting the individual test may assist the student and provide an effective route to success. For instance, a student might find written tests with larger amounts of white space less confusing to read.

2. *Observation.* Teachers can observe students' daily progress and keep detailed records of their findings. These can be collected, documented on log sheets or other graphic organizers, and then presented at parent conferences.

3. *Interviews.* Talking with children about their development permits teachers to combine their own assessments with students' perceptions. Interviews also provide an opportunity to discuss students' expectations and desires for the rest of the school year.

4. *Assessment and grading.* Caution must be followed to motivate low-achieving students. Use minor methods such as not using red pen to correct; instead, highlight areas of both strengths and weaknesses. Try to write a comment here and there. In class, the teacher should always praise all students, as well as have each student praise each other in class by clapping or giving a partner a "highfive." The key words are *flexibility* and *change* when reaching our nation's urban, diverse, and very challenging student population.

INSTRUCTIONAL RESOURCES FOR DIVERSE STUDENTS

Inclusive classrooms offer potential advantages. According to Athanases et al. (1995), diverse classrooms are more like the real world that students will need to appreciate and in which they need to respond appropriately when they are working in a community across the nation. They will be less afraid of others who are different and will be more likely to value the contributions of all people. Diverse, urban students can be taught to be more tolerant of others, more aware of the needs of others, and better able to communicate. Students will learn to make their own decisions and become friends with those who are different from them, even when others are critical. Lastly, students in a diverse classroom often become advocates for all people from all cultures as well as those with disabilities and challenges exhibited in the classroom.

Although the challenges presented by a diverse student body, including varied ability levels, have always been in the nation's classrooms, schools are now assuming the responsibility of providing instruction to help all students succeed. The classroom setting should promote inclusion and acceptance of cultural differences. The schools' climate and instructional programs that accommodate and celebrate student diversity promote the highest achievement for all students.

Students' progress toward success also involves a natural immersion in *authentic* resources. All learners, including those at risk of failing, benefit from literacy-rich classrooms with easy access to paperbacks, anthologies, fiction and nonfiction works, dramas, comedies, poetry, illustration books, BIG books, how-to manuals, talking books, books on the Internet, magazines, newspapers, and comic books. Students are more apt to respond positively to these materials when they are permitted to choose from a wide variety of options. They will especially enjoy this immersion when they observe teachers respecting their choices and when they are encouraged to read at their own comfortable pace and space in the classroom.

Schools are organized to provide instruction for all students. This can be a difficult task, and teachers need consistent support from administrators, parents, and each other. Administrative support is an invaluable resource for teachers as they struggle to identify and respond to diverse students' needs. Staff training can offer help by making time for learning and sharing with other teachers. One way of ensuring teacher–teacher coordination is through collaborative efforts.

The use of collaborative efforts is important when trying to reach a diverse population. Collaboration is the involvement of teachers in the planning, implementation, and evaluation of new instructional techniques. Staff members who help plan inclusion efforts may be more enthusiastic about making them succeed for each student.

Wood and Long (1994) reviewed eight ways to embrace teacher collaboration in diversity classroom programs.

1. *Communicate.* Talk openly and honestly about the differences and similarities among your students. Discuss how you can learn from each other's unique experiences and abilities.

2 *Accept.* Strive to identify and eliminate your own prejudices and personal biases. Consider joining a teacher support group to talk about changing attitudes.

3. *Understand.* Realize that all students are different. Work to understand each child's special gifts and needs.

4. *Individualize.* When possible, plan learning activities that are matched to the individual learning needs and abilities of each child. For example, learning centers can help students with different learning styles and abilities meet the same objectives.

5. *Personalize.* Use classroom decorations and displays that reflect and celebrate the diversity in your school and the world. Make sure the physical space of the classroom is adapted to the needs of all students.

6. *Connect.* Create classroom activities that help diverse students interact and learn from one another. Encourage students with diverse backgrounds and skills to work together on small-group projects. Offer clubs such as the Minority Achievement Program to explore and celebrate the diverse backgrounds of all minorities at your school.

7. *Encourage.* Express confidence in all students' abilities. Let each child know that you believe he or she can succeed.

8. *Utilize technology.* Computer technology, as previously stated, can offer children equal opportunities for success, give assistance to children with special challenges, and create a setting for appropriate social interaction.

DIVERSITY IN THE CURRICULUM: PRACTICAL APPLICATION

Sheppo et al. (1995) described how an urban school deals with diversity in their curricula. Lincoln School, a center for fifth and sixth grade students in Springfield, Illinois, serves an area that encompasses all income levels, from the most expensive subdivision in the city to public housing projects. Approximately one-third of the students are ethnic minorities, and two-fifths receive free or reduced-price lunch. Twenty percent of the students have mild to moderate disabilities, and over 40% of the students at Lincoln School also exhibit some degree of behavior problems. Here, all teachers work in collaborative teams to provide an inclusive curriculum and learning environment for almost 400 diverse students through a site-based initiative called Project LINCOL'N (Living in the New Computer Oriented Learning 'Nvironment). The vision of Project LINCOL'N is to enable all students, including students with challenges in behavior or academics, to engage in authentic learning in a problem-solving environment. To make this happen, the school adopted three agendas for reform.

First, educators created an integrated curriculum that allows students to focus on carefully selected themes and concepts (Lewis, 1990). Second, students became active learners, constructing their own knowledge and understanding through the interaction and support of people (Sheingold, 1991). Third, multimedia technologies were incorporated into the curriculum because they had significant potential for supporting an integrated curriculum and for encouraging active student learning (Willis, 1992).

The use of an integrated curriculum is key to including all students in the learning process. Students use the knowledge they have gained in each subject to help put their group's final project together. Subject areas such as science or math can have integrated themes and lessons built into the core curriculum. Let's consider how Project LINCOL'N employed integrative themes in curricula for science, social studies, mathematics, literacy, and special areas/electives.

Science

With science, students developed a knowledge base about the basic composition of living things (e.g., cell, kingdoms of living things, and biomes through hands-on activities and video-enhanced instruction that included a laser disc-based science series). Depending on their abilities, students used several types of reference materials from the science textbook, to electronic encyclopedias, to research from the Internet. There were also a standard electronic encyclopedia and a high interest/lower reading level encyclopedia with an easy-to-use feature for taking notes. One student used an integrative computer laser disc program to discover desert animals' behavioral and structural adaptations. Her clips from the laser disc illustrated the group's oral presentation.

Social Studies

In the area of social studies, sixth graders focused on world geography as they surveyed the continents of our living world. Activities such as the "Seven-Day Travel Tour" emphasized map reading and research skills. Teams planned an itinerary that included five locations in three countries in Europe or Asia. Students had to locate information about climate and physical features of different countries, designate tourist attractions at each stop, and discover at least one interesting recipe. To access the Internet, students used Mosaic, a graphical interface that makes the complex network easier to use.

The hypertext-based information browser saves addresses of places worth visiting, allowing students to go on electronic expeditions to locations preset by teachers on the basis of individual student's abilities. Using other software, students developed travel brochures, newsletters, video travelogues, or computer/laser disc programs selling their tours. One student used her new research and map skills to complete her portion of the project, she compared the geography of the desert regions of North America and Africa.

Mathematics

In math, students started with reviewing numeration systems and place value in whole and decimal numbers. Students then used data collection, graphing, and problem-solving strategies while working on their culminating project. In an extension activity, students gathered information on local weather conditions from the newspaper, entered it into a database, and analyzed computer-generated graphs. Using different computer applications, from a simple program that limits data and focuses on basic graphs to a more sophisticated program that utilizes spreadsheets and multiple variables, allowed all students to learn the math concepts while practicing at a level appropriate to them. One student developed double bar graphs to compare seasonal temperature ranges between the desert and our own deciduous forest biome and triple line graphs to compare yearly rainfall in three desert regions around the world.

Literacy

In the area of literature, reading books such as the *Black Pearl* by Scott O'Dell or *Kon-Tiki* by Thor Heyerdahl stimulates student discussion about the characters' actions, beliefs, reactions, and concerns about the environment. Students cultivated *reading strategies,* such as skimming and scanning for information. They also created *writing strategies,* such as comparing, contrasting, describing. and forming literature circles. Students practiced these strategies while reading books that were on their own level but still reflected the curricular theme. Both the special education and regular education teachers monitored several reading groups, and together they led class discussions that involved all students.

Special Areas/Electives

In other elective or special areas such as art, this concept can continue to be implemented. An art class used features of the various biomes as the subject of a project. Students painted one feature twice, using first cool colors and then warm colors to convey mood. One student prepared a sketchbook illustrating the structural adaptations cacti use to survive in the desert and analyzed them in an accompanying text.

Students may choose from a variety of ways to demonstrate what they learn, depending on their strengths and learning styles. Possible options for authentic classroom performance might include written reports, videotapes, displays, computer-processed reports with clipart and other visual enhancements. Also, each group can select a special way of demonstrating its new knowledge, skills, and learning strategies and present the projects at a bimonthly Parents' Night. When teachers evaluate these culminating projects, they do so with an understanding of each student's strengths and weaknesses.

Through portfolio assessment, teachers, parents, and students evaluate progress in all academic subject areas and set goals for future growth. Both the structure of the curriculum and the use of multimedia technologies allow us to challenge students and to modify for students with special challenges.

To celebrate our urban children living in a culturally diverse community, the classrooms should have a different look and feel about them. There should be an absence of traditional, neat rows of desks. An observer would see desks in groups of four to encourage student interaction. Students have responsibilities such as homework collector (for group only), computer maintenance (keeps the computers in tidy shape), or classroom computer technician (boot all computers up in the morning and sign off every evening), maintaining jobs that affect all students in each classroom. Many students do not remain seated; they are grouped or huddled around a computer, hunched over tables filled with reference books, and sit on the floor planning, storyboarding, organizing, and communicating. Teachers, too, huddle, hunch, and sit on the floor as they facilitate groups. The noise level is often high, but listen in on each group and hear the discussions. Students and teachers are focused, on-task, and excited about teaching and learning. Project LINCOL'N can become *any* urban school in the United States.

The concepts and applications of Project LINCOL'N are readily employable in urban schools across the nation. Integration of curriculum and alternative ideas about instruction, grouping, and problem solving will promote effective student learning. Inclusive classrooms offer other potential advantages. In short, the challenges presented by a diverse student body warrant revisons in curricula compatible with student needs and yet consistent with canons of basic learning universal to all students.

6

Effective Approaches for Schoolwide and Classroom Behavior Management

Nancy R. Macciomei

The most demanding tasks of educators is dealing with daily disruptive behavior challenges. According to Kerr and Nelson (1998), students who are chronically defiant, disruptive, aggressive, and noncomplaint or engage in nonfunctional behaviors pose extreme challenges to teachers and administrators. Educators who work with such students, however, must ultimately manage them in group settings. Establishing a productive and orderly classroom and school environment in which to focus on target behaviors is the key to any behavioral approach. The purpose of this chapter is to discuss options available for effective approaches toward behavior management and to offer skills necessary to create productive learning environments with minimal disruptions.

FIRST APPROACH: APPROPRIATE AND FUNCTIONAL CURRICULA

Many crisis situations can be prevented through careful assessment, effective educational programming, and behavioral support. With this in mind, classroom management should be viewed as a set of proactive strategies that reduce the need for selected interventions for a large number of students. The most essential prerequisites to effective classroom approaches are an *appropriate* and *functional* academic curriculum that includes effective instructional practices (Shores, Gunter et al., 1993; Suga, 1995). Appropriate and functional curricula must meet the students' individual needs and *be perceived by the students as important and meaningful. A curriculum that is poorly matched to students' aptitudes and interests is likely to be aversive, therefore setting the scene for avoidance behaviors.*

The following questions make up an informal checklist that the teacher can use to assess the potential source of problem behaviors and key into the approach to the daily lessons:

1. Is what I am teaching useful or important to the students?

2. Do the students know what I expect them to do?

3. Are there any obstacles to the students' performing as desired?

4. Do I need to use differentiated instruction for specific students due to very high or low ability levels?

5. What are the consequences of *desired performance*?

6. What are the consequences of nonperformance?

7. When does the problem behavior occur?

8. What is different about students who are not displaying the problem behavior?

9. How can I change my instruction to help students develop the skill(s) I am trying to teach?

Effective Teaching: The Best Approach

The least intrusive and most natural behavior management approaches are good teaching practices. Effective teaching indicates that best practices include brisk instructional pacing, reviewing students' work frequently, giving systematic and constructive corrective feedback, minimizing pupil errors, providing guided practice, modeling new behaviors, providing transitions between lessons or concepts, and monitoring student performance (Bickel & Bickle, 1986; Kameenui & Darch, 1995; Rosenshine & Stevens, 1986). Each teacher and administrator must decide what degree of intervention is best for his or her particular population. The most appropriate context for a classroom behavior management approach is a schoolwide disciplinary plan that connects the teacher's strategy with expectations and consequences that exist throughout the school building. Here are two examples of schoolwide discipline programs utilizing fundamental behavioral interventions.

The Catch 'Em Being Good Program

The Catch 'Em Being Good Program is a positive approach to initiating and maintaining motivation toward good behavior throughout the school building and throughout the school day. All adult staff members should be involved, letting students know that their appropriate behaviors should continue through the day. This approach also lets children know that their appropriate behavior is important to, and noticed and appreciated by, all at the school. Children love earning Catch 'Em Being Good Rewards to collect or redeem for privileges or prizes.

Getting Started

Create rewards such as tickets, tokens, buttons, or stamps and stack them in convenient bundles. Depending on the technology at the school, the school logo or mascot could be printed on each item. The rewards should be accessible to all staff members, keeping a handful in pockets for instant use during the day. All teachers and staff have the rewards on them throughout the day. The explanation of earning the tangible rewards is given to the children on the first day of school as well as explained in the school handbook. Staff must keep in mind that the rewards (tickets, etc.) would be used on a variable schedule. They should try not to be too predictable, so that children will never know when they will be rewarded.

Earning Tickets/Tokens

A committee or Parent-Teacher Association (PTA) will determine the worth (number of tickets) of each item for sale in the school store. Tickets should be handed out by staff based on one or more of the following criteria:

1. *Cooperative behavior in the classroom.* Examples of cooperative behaviors would be offering to help another student, giving a compliment, sharing materials, helping with cleanup, and greeting visitors politely.

2. *Good work habits.* The teacher may staple or attach the reward (ticket, token, etc.) on a student's paper showing neatness, accuracy, improvement, correct spelling, handing homework in on time, and maintaining an orderly deck.

3. *Participation.* All staff distribute rewards for displaying good sportsmanship, teamwork, group discussions, respecting school property, safe handling of lab equipment, accuracy and responsibility in handling tickets/tokens. Providers of tokens include support staff members such as cafeteria workers, maintenance people, and bus drivers.

4. *Appropriate behaviors as a group.* Examples may include a good day with a substitute teacher, being ready to begin class when the bell rings, all morning work completed on time (by everyone!), quietly lining up for specials (physical education, art, music, etc.), walking quietly in the hall to the cafeteria, low, inside voices in the cafeteria, and respect during field trip activities. The teacher can keep a glass jar for group tickets or tokens and then use the tickets for group rewards.

5. *Any particular behavior that promotes manners, good citizenship, and honesty.* Examples may be raising a hand to ask questions, responding with thank you or yes, sir/ma'am, *and using grammatically correct language over slang.*

6. *Admitting to minor problems and owning fault.* This includes voluntarily and receptively admitting fault when blamed by teachers and administrators. Omission of defensive, deflective, or argumentative actions shows self-recognition of the student's imperfections and willingness to accept constructive criticism.

Donations for the School Store

Students can redeem their tickets or tokens at the school store on specific days and times. The PTA president and PTA members, as well as the discipline committee members, help to keep the store stocked with donations from community businesses and individuals. The store can be run by student council members, safety patrol, or other responsible student groups in the school.

Keeping the Tickets or Tokens Safe and Ready to Spend

Tickets or tokens should be given to students throughout the day. However, each classroom should have a ticket or token collector, recorder, and bank tellers to distribute on days of purchasing. The students should receive a receipt or count of current tickets that they have earned. Accountancy of earned tokens, incidentally, is best during math lessons. Addition, subtraction, money skills, and story problems can be used to integrate the schoolwide approach as part of the functional curriculum.

Weekly Drawings

To offer a greater incentive, there can be a weekly raffle drawing, for a "big-ticket item." Lottery-like winners are announced during the morning news or announcements. This can take place once a week or once a month.

Stoplight Method for Classroom Behavior Management

Elementary-wide interventions may seem facile because of the amenable nature of younger learners. Kindergarten to fifth grade urban students may be in early stages of behavioral disorders and receptive to consistently structured programming over their high school cohorts. At Oaklawn Elementary School (1997–98), for example, geographically situated "uptown" of Charlotte, North Carolina, systemwide strategies for behavior control existed for in-class and out-of-class instructors using the "stoplight method." Simply employing three colors of a stoplight (red, yellow, and green), teachers constructed a poster board with a pocket for each student in the classroom. In each pocket were three strips of paper—green, yellow, and red. Pulling each strip signals to the student a series of disciplinary steps.

Green Strip

When the green strip is pulled, the teacher must follow two steps. First, use private responses. This involves talking to the student about the specific inappropriate behavior and listening to the student's concerns. Teachers clearly identify desired or appropriate behaviors expected of the student and provide opportunities for subsequent demonstration of that behavior. Second, the teacher redirects the student toward another task. This entails overlooking the student's hostility and defensiveness while diverting attention to on-task activities.

Yellow Strip

When the yellow strip is pulled, teachers begin documenting on a log sheet the behavior offense and interventions employed. Yellow strips mean an immediate consequence is necessary as well as a phone call home before the day is over. Among the following consequences against students are:

- Loss of immediate privileges (e.g., free time, isolated lunch)
- Overcorrection (cleanup of child's mess and other cleanup duty)
- Short-term time-out (5–10 minutes)
- Child writes note to parent explaining mistake made

- Teacher calls home
- Child writes apology letter to children offended by his or her action

Concurrent to signaling punitive consequences, teachers receive explicit instructions and must record frequency of rewarding students for appropriate actions and signs of improving classroom participation.

Red Strip

When the red strip is pulled, it means immediate and harsher consequences are necessary to help student restore self-control. Teachers are carefully advised to avoid taking offenses personally and to maintain the dignity of students despite outrageous classroom disruptions or ostensible disrespect for the teacher's authority. Consequences selected by teachers for red-strip action include:

1. Time-out in another room (no longer than 15 minutes).
2. In-class isolation (ICI). Use of ICI requires notification to parents of the method and reasons for use.
3. Call the office. Failure of the child to restore composure or engage in target behaviors may warrant immediately calling the office. Teachers are admonished not to send children to the office given their potential hallway and schoolwide disturbances. Assistant principals or designated authority then report to the classroom for intervention.

Overall, research has shown that schoolwide discipline approaches are extremely effective (Colvin et al., 1993; Nelson et al., 1995). Reasons cited are obvious and consistent with underlying tenets of conditioning theory. For example, most children like to be told when they are doing something right. Students tend to respond appropriately when classroom atmosphere is upbeat, and teachers are friendly. More importantly, favorable responses especially are high when token-delivery is reliable and predictable.

However, there is a difference between positive feedback and encouragement. Dreikurs et al. (1982) states that the primary difference is that positive feedback *often provides some judgment from the teacher about the appropriateness of the behavior, whereas encouragement recognizes the behavior but does not provide judgment from the teacher.* An example of positive feedback is a teacher saying, "I like the way Nancy is waiting in line quietly." An example of encouragement is to say, "I'm sure that you know how to stand in line." Both encouragement and positive feedback are effective procedures for noticing what is positive about the behavior of students.

While seemingly an innocuous point, differential uses of positive remarks can significantly increase or decrease student reactions. Students who are explicitly told what their appropriate behavior is and reinforced for it (e.g., positive feedback) immediately receive incentives to repeat the target behavior in the future. They undergo contingency-shaped conditioning, where behavior and consequence are made explicit and simultaneous to their appropriate behavior. With encouragement, desired behaviors are taught by rule-governed behaviors. Here the teacher *assumes the student knows how to respond appropriately and the inherent consequences received for doing so.* Rule-governed conditioning may be faster but is seriously ineffective for high-risk and maladaptively behaving students who are regularly noncompliant and follow very few external school rules. This is because overt noncompliance of "if-then" conditions suggests weak motivation for consequences and history of impulsive action despite the outcomes. Consequently, poor overt instruction-following behaviors predicts extremely poor covert instruction-following behaviors. Their abilities for internally dictated rules governing behavior are extremely low and unreliable for learning (Ruben, 1992, 1998).

Token Economy Systems in the Classroom

Token economy programs have been successful in altering disruptive behaviors such as shouting out answers during instruction, and off-task behavior. Token economy programs (Kerr & Nelson, 1998) repeatedly have been successful in increasing attention and academic performance. As clearly shown, the basic objective of token economy is *delayed reinforcement.* Earned tokens are symbols for potential rewards they are later traded in for. Tokens increase behavior duration for hours until a long chain of appropriate action receives reinforcers. Tokens are exchanged midday or end of day for conditioned or unconditioned reinforcers such as food, money, or privileges and thereby encourage repetition of long chains of appropriate behaviors on subsequent days. Successful token programs clearly post what the "exchange rate" is for redeemable tokens. That way, students remain aware of token values and may emit behaviors not so much for the token but for what the token earns them later on.

To begin token programs, basic materials are necessary. These include many, but not all, of the following: reinforcers desired by the classroom, a kitchen timer, record data sheet, and different types of tokens. Briefly reviewed are key components of token economy programs.

Tokens

Tokens are items (e.g., tickets, chips, play money, points) that can be exchanged for something of value. Use tokens to reward groups or teams that are behaving appropriately in class. Also, allow groups or individuals to accumulate tokens they can spend on privileges such as no homework or free time. Also, a school or classroom store can be set up with donations from community businesses for students to spend their tokens.

Tangibles

Tangibles are rewards or objects that students want or need, including objects they can consume. Elementary students love pencils, crayons, paper, erasers, superballs, stickers, and juice. Middle school students love hygienic products such as deodorant, cologne, perfume, as well as balls (e.g., footballs, basketballs, soccer balls), comic books, mirrors, combs, brushes, hair picks, lip gloss, wallets, and edibles, especially soda pop. Tokens can be exchanged for tangible reinforcers; the bigger the reinforcer, the more tokens it will take for the exchange. Tangible reinforcers may be needed to maintain the behavior of a student or of the whole class for meeting a class goal. The class may earn a class soccer ball by pooling their tokens.

More suggestions for tangible reinforcements to stock in the school store are as follows: address books, art supplies, audiocassette tapes, badges, Beannie Babies, beanbags, books, bookmarks, calendars, colored paper, computer paper, comic books, coloring books, cosmetics, crayons, grab bags, jacks, jump ropes, erasers, key chains, miniature cars, CD's, toothbrushes, stuffed animals, wax lips and teeth, and yo-yos.

Approaches to Verbal Reprimands

Reprimanding students for inappropriate behaviors has been the norm in the field of teaching. Verbal reprimands get tricky, however, because teacher interpretations may vary, and definitions of acceptable feedback may be liberal or conservative based on school demographics. Advocates of corrective feedback (O'Leary et al., 1970; Van Houten et al., 1982) operationally qualify reprimands according to safe and reliable guidelines. These include:

1. *Make reprimands private not public.* Humiliating or embarrassing a student is likely to increase that student's resentment and may create an unsafe situation. Teachers who raise their voice repeatedly desensitize students to reprimands. Students may be more inclined to listen to what you are saying when you use a normal speaking voice.

2. *Look at the student when speaking.* Direct contact with the student is essential. Insisting on eye contact by the student, however, is cautioned given that many students' cultures may frown on eye contact.

3. *Stand near the student while talking to him or her.* A good idea with children is to remain at least one leg-length away from the student and honor that individual's personal space needs.

4. *Do not point a finger at the student.* Teachers need to consciously remember not to point at students.

5. *Do not insist on having the last word.* Having the last word may turn into a power struggle. Make a statement and stop the conversation.

6. *What is said and not said.* This may be the most powerful approach for altering behaviors. A loud speaking voice that commands students' attention without screaming is the long-term goal for all individuals who work in public schools. All educators and administrators can have an authoritative, but courteous, voice. Nonverbal cues unintentionally, but forceably, exhibited may interfere with the efficacy of corrective reprimands. Staub (1987) states that 80% of the language received by an individual in a stressful situation is nonverbal.

Likewise, Johns and Carr (1995) have identified a number of common negative behavior management techniques that frequently, but ineffectively, are used in classrooms. These include:

1. Forcing students to do something they don't want to do.
2. Forcing students to admit to lies.
3. Demanding confessions from students.
4. Using confrontational techniques.
5. Asking students why they act out.
6. Punishing students in a punitive manner.
7. Making disapproving or negative comments.
8. Comparing a student's behavior with other students' behavior.
9. Yelling at students.
10. Engaging in verbal power struggles.
11. Making unrealistic threats.
12. Ridiculing students.

Sugai (1995) observed that teachers' behavioral expectations often were considerably above students' abilities to perform. He recommended that after pinpointing the identified behaviors that are expected, decide what behaviors are achievable and proceed to shaping.

Shaping

Shaping has a long history of proven effectiveness in classroom application. Jones and Carr (1995) echo pioneer researchers by their instructional advice on shaping techniques. First is to identify students' current behavioral level. Selected behaviors to be shaped are ones students demonstrate rather than ones they "ought to demonstrate." Shaping proceeds through a simple series of antecedent prompts and reinforcers. Students prompted to respond know immediately the consequence received for responding. As target responses occur, criteria for the reinforcer vary. First the child, for example, spends 5 minutes quietly sitting in exchange for positive teacher attention. Now, the response criterion is up to 10 minutes for the same reinforcer. Varying the response criterion and reinforcer is also called *differential reinforcement*. As criteria change, so does the reinforcement schedule. Early steps of shaping may deliver the reinforcer immediately after so many minutes of target sitting. By altering reinforcement, delivery may be *every time or every other time the student sits; or delivery may be exactly after so many minutes or after an average amount of minutes elapse.* In the former case, reinforcement delivery is on a *fixed or variable rate schedule. Rate means amount of behavior.* In the latter case, reinforcement delivery is on a *fixed or variable interval schedule. Interval refers to time or duration of behavior.*

Gresham and Reschly (1988) stated that the specific management goals expressed by teachers are likely to include increasing such desired student behaviors as attending to tasks, remaining in-seat, following teacher directions, using time productively, and giving correct academic responses. Teachers are also concerned about altering behaviors that are dangerous, disruptive, or incompatible with the completion of academic tasks. Educators' and administrators' expectations are more likely to be accepted if they consider the dynamics and expectations of the students. Much of classroom misbehavior is attributable to inappropriate classroom behavior management. This refers to students who have been reinforced for their tantrums, defying authority, aggressive acts against others, or being noncompliant when others of the same developmental age do not demonstrate such behaviors.

Power Struggles

According to Shores, Gunter et al. (1993) a common, almost impulsive effort toward behavior control is power struggles between the teacher and students. Like adults, children react negatively to confrontational measures. If students sense that the teacher is reacting from frustration or feels out of control of the situation, they may respond with even more intensive, inappropriate behaviors. The behavior management approach must be thoughtfully chosen, involve student input, and have a positive approach for most consequences.

Two other mistakes are made, even by master teachers. The first is to assume that students know what is expected of them. An indication of this problem is the absence of clear rules and procedures. Either the rules are nonexistent, or they are worded too vaguely (e.g., use good manners, respect others). The second mistake is to punish students for their failure to demonstrate a behavior that they do not know how to perform (e.g., follow directions, remaining in-seat). Although noncompliance and opposition may reflect a student's decision not to follow a direction, it may also indicate that the student does not know what behavior is expected, that there are obstacles to the student's performing as desired, or that the student lacks the skills to exhibit the desired behavior. Therefore, before punitive measures are given, the administrator or educator must be sure that the student can perform the requested task.

Setting Limits

Brophy (1988) states that effective management of student behavior requires clearly specified guidelines with consequences when students do not follow those guidelines. Guidelines in the classroom consist of procedures and rules. Procedures are classroom routines that occur at specified times and allow the classroom to run effectively. These procedures need to be taught to students and used consistently so that the classroom runs smoothly. Each teacher needs to establish procedures for record keeping (e.g., attendance), passing out paper and materials, storing materials and books, collecting papers and materials, entering and leaving the room (alone and with the class) and making the transition between tasks. Rules provide the structure for acceptable and unacceptable classroom behaviors. According to Emmer et al. (1989), instead of trying to develop a rule to govern every possible misbehavior, teachers should develop a few general rules that guide students in determining whether behavior is or is not acceptable. These rules should be based on the teacher's criteria for what constitutes a behavior problem. Some teachers involve students in determining class rules and consequences. This approach, along with class meetings, is discussed later in this chapter.

Examples of general classroom rules are as follows:

1. Raise your hand if you have something to contribute.
2. Do not interfere with the learning of your classmates.
3. Do not interfere with the teacher's instruction.
4. Complete tasks and homework on time.
5. Do not bring to school materials (e.g., toys, action figures, beeping house key chains or virtual pets/Tamagotchis) that interfere with your learning.
6. Keep hands and feet to yourself.

These rules should be posted, in large, clear letters, in at least three areas within the classroom and referred to quite often. Recalling rules through simple verbal reprimands is one common approach. But Ferrara (1987) employed innovative ways to prompt disorderly students to pay attention to classroom rules without disrupting lesson plans or isolating the students. Such creativity included:

1. Give simple negative feedback. In this case, the student is told that the solution is not quite right and is encouraged to try again. The student can also be praised for effort.
2. Refresh working memory. Repeat parts of the problem verbatim and discuss the known quantities.
3. Use numerals as memory aids. Ask students to write down the quantities they know, based on information provided in the text.
4. Provide a transfer hint. Ask students to think about a similar problem they have done. Students can provide the example of the similar problem.
5. Provide a demonstration and rationale. Provide all the information to solve the problem and an explanation or rationale for it.
6. Give a strategic-orientation hint. Encourage the students to apply the information they have just learned to other types of problems.

The teacher should express confidence that all students will comply with rules and procedures. Administrators and teachers should always remember to praise desired behaviors. After a new rule has been introduced or learned to mastery, point out the times students follow it. Always praise using content-specific language, for example, "Thank you for being quiet while I was talking." Lastly, hold students accountable after they have mastered the rules and procedures.

Contracting

Allen et al. (1983) explain that a written description of contingencies is called contracting. Contracting is a useful procedure for all ages of students. It clearly specifies target behaviors expected of students in exchange for the rewards they will receive. Preagreements between teacher and student on terms of contracting prevent later discordance over performance expectation and particularly over choice of reinforcers. General guidelines for implementing a contingency contract might include:

1. Explain to the student what a contract is and how it works. The explanation should be appropriately stated for the student's ability level. It is important to give examples and show sample contracts.

2. Ask the student to suggest tasks that might be included in a contract between student and teacher. Write these down.

3. Suggest tasks that you would like to see the student accomplish, and write these down.

4. Decide on mutually agreeable tasks. Any third party involved in the contract should also agree on the tasks that you have selected.

5. Discuss with the student possible activities, items, or privileges that the student would like to earn. Write these down.

6. Negotiate how the student will earn the reinforcers by accomplishing portions or all of the tasks.

7. Identify the criteria for mastery of each task (time allotted, achievement level, how the task is to be evaluated).

8. Determine when the student will receive the reinforcers for completing tasks.

9. Determine when the contract will be reviewed to make necessary revisions or to note progress.

10. Make an extra copy of the contract. Give this copy to the student and any third party involved.

11. Sign the contract; get the student to sign the contract; and if there is a third party involved, ask the third party to sign the contract.

Rhode et al. (1993), in addition, suggested natural positive reinforcers, such as the following:

- Access to lunchroom snack machines
- Attend school dances, assemblies, plays, performances (band, etc.)
- Be first in line (to anywhere!)
- Care for class pets
- Decorate the classroom
- Eat lunch outside or in another place rather than the cafeteria
- Eat lunch with a special person
- Help the custodian

- Pass out papers
- Run errands
- Serve as class or office messenger
- Sharpen class pencils
- Sit by a friend or special person
- Tutor in class or with younger students
- Water class plants

Life-Space Interviewing

The life-space interview (LSI) originally was discussed by Wood and Long (1994). These researchers describe this approach to help students with emotional challenges cope with a crisis situation. There are two primary goals. First is to provide emotional first aid so that the student can regain composure and restore normal activity level as soon as possible. Second is to take advantage of the conflict situation to assist students in resolving their own personal conflicts. Long et al. (1980) discussed the following suggestions for the application of the life-space interview by teachers and administrators:

1. To calm students or chill them out and shake off the anger, use humor and physical activity (running laps, basketball), then allow students to talk about the issue.

2. Be as courteous as you would be if you were dealing with a friend or another adult. Give the student time to adequately explain his or her side of the story and listen attentively. If you ask questions, be sure to give the student time to think and respond to them.

3. Conduct the life-space interview in as private a place as possible. No one wants to exhibit problems, throw tantrums, or be extremely upset in front of others. Find a private, quiet place to conduct the session.

4. Eliminate barriers between you and the student. Position yourself at eye level. With a young child, pull up small chairs and sit down so that you are at the same level.

5. Ask the student to provide his or her interpretation of the event, first. Listen carefully and be sure that you clarify any misunderstandings. But do not give in to his or her misperceptions of the situation. Confront the student, if necessary, to point out that there is another way to view the situation.

6. Discuss what needs to be done to resolve the situation. If an apology is needed, role play and rehearse how that can be done. If the conflict needs to be further discussed and resolved with another person, plan procedures for doing so before crisis situations occur.

7. Avoid invalidating students' feelings by claiming that they could not possibly feel the way they say they do. Students with emotional or behavior challenges often say outrageous things that they mean at the time. Listen carefully without judging or denying their feelings. Allow time for students to ask you questions and to prepare a follow-up.

THE POSITIVE APPROACH

Teachers frequently need to change their own behavior in order to change the behavior of students. According to Hunter (1982), not only do teachers identify classroom management as a cause of stress, but many also cite it as their reason for leaving the profession. When teachers are asked to look for positive behaviors of children, they respond with, "there aren't any!" The poor behaviors far out-weighed the good. Teachers and administrators get into the habit of noticing and calling attention to misbehavior instead of noticing appropriate behaviors. Class-room teachers must look for, and say something positive to, students who are per-forming appropriate behaviors.

The Theory of Positive Discipline

The desire for dignity and respect is not only a part of school life for staff and students but a very important part of our society. Educators need to be aware of the significance of this desire and realize that cooperation based on mutual respect is more effective than authoritarian control (Nelson, 1987). There need to be oppor-tunities provided for children to experience responsibility at school, due to a lack of it within the home and community. Otherwise, they become dependent recipi-ents who feel the only way to achieve belonging and significance is by manipulating other people. In her book *Positive Discipline*, Nelson (1987) describes positive dis-cipline as an approach that is effective in teaching children self-discipline, respon-sibility, cooperation, and problem-solving skills. This approach is not humiliating to children or adults.

Authoritative control usually involves punishment that is humiliating to chil-dren. Permissiveness is certainly humiliating to adults. Positive discipline is based on a mutual respect and cooperation that incorporate firmness with dignity and respect. There are long-range results of current punitive practices that children feel, or what Nelson refers to as the *four Rs of punishment*:

1. Resentment—*This is unfair. I can't trust adults!*
2. Revenge—*They will regret this. I'll get them!*
3. Rebellion—*I'll do the opposite to prove I am right!*
4. Retreat—(Sneakiness)—*I won't get caught next time*—or (reduced self-esteem)—*I am a bad person.*

It is possible that misbehavior might get worse when positive discipline skills are first used. However, educators notice that there is a leveling off before the child misbehaves again. Misbehavior becomes less intense, with longer leveling-off peri-ods, when the positive discipline approach is used consistently. When educators use firmness and consistency with dignity and respect, children soon learn that their misbehavior does not get the results they expect, and they may be motivated to change their behavior.

One important concept about positive discipline is that children are more willing to follow rules that they have helped establish. They become effective decision makers with healthy self-concepts when they learn to be contributing members of a classroom family and of the school society. Six basic concepts, taken from Adlerian theory, are essential in understanding the positive discipline approach:

1. *Children are social beings.* Behavior is determined within a social context. Children make decisions about themselves and their behavior based on how they see themselves in relationship to others. Also, they see themselves in relationship to how they think others feel about them.

2. *Behavior is goal-oriented.* Behavior is based on a goal to be achieved and maintained in a situation.

3. *A child's primary goal is to belong and to be significant.* The goal of all behavior is to achieve belonging and significance within the social environment.

4. *A misbehaving child is a discouraged child.* Usually, a misbehaving child acts inappropriately, so it is easy to understand why it is difficult for most adults to get past the behavior.

5. *Social interest.* Have real concern for one's fellow person and a sincere desire to make a contribution to society.

6. *Equality.* All people have equal claims to dignity and respect.

These six basic concepts provide the foundation for understanding behavior and developing the attitudes and techniques necessary to implement the positive discipline approach. Positive discipline also entails viewing students as potential *good behavers instead of repeat offenders.* While their school records may be replete with perennial mischief, stereotyping a student as permanently delinquent and nonrehabilitative squelches teacher incentive and may sabotage use of positive approaches. In this respect, Glenn and Nelson (1987) identify seven significant perceptions and skills necessary for developing capable people:

1. Strong perceptions of personal capabilities (*I am capable*).

2. Strong perceptions of significance in primary relationships (*I contribute in meaningful ways and I am genuinely needed*).

3. Strong perceptions of personal power or influence over life (*I can influence what happens to me*).

4. Strong intrapersonal skills; the ability to understand personal emotions and to use that understanding to develop self-discipline and self-control.

5. Strong interpersonal skills; the ability to work with others and develop friendships through communication, cooperation, negotiation, sharing, empathizing, and listening.

6. Strong systemic skills; the ability to respond to the limits and consequences of everyday life with responsibility, adaptability, flexibility, and integrity.

7. Strong judgmental skills; the ability to use wisdom and to evaluate situations according to the appropriate values.

Most misbehavior can be traced to a lack of development in these seven perceptions and skills. Today, children do not have many opportunities to feel needed and significant, but teachers can provide these opportunities on a daily basis.

Positive Discipline: Effective Approaches

There is never one way to alter behavior problems with children. However, the following remedies for effective responses are the backbone of the positive discipline approach.

Class Meetings

Most problems can be solved in a class meeting that is led by the classroom teacher. The purposes of class meetings are to give compliments, to help each other, to solve problems, and to plan events. Many teachers start every meeting by asking the children, What are the two main purposes of our class meetings? The two main purposes are to help each other and to solve problems. This should be stated at the beginning of every class meeting.

Giving Compliments

Nelson (1987) states that the teacher should spend some time with children exploring the meaning of compliments. This can be done informally during the first class meeting. Compliments should consist of acknowledgment of others in the following areas: (1) accomplishments, (2) helpfulness, and (3) sharing.

Have the children brainstorm for specific examples in each of these areas. Then teach them to use the words, "I would like to compliment Nancy for . . ." Using these consistent phrases helps children stay on the task of recognizing what others do, rather than what they wear. The teacher should always start by giving several compliments (from notes taken during the day of children who would merit recognition). The teacher should model giving compliments, making sure they eventually cover every child in the classroom. It is also a good practice to teach the students to say thank you after receiving a compliment.

Teach Cause and Effect

Before children can solve class problems, they must understand the nature of cause and effect. Teach the students to use logical consequences before trying to solve any problem. Start by having them brainstorm simple cause-and-effect situations such as, If you don't sleep? (You get tired). Explain that consequences have to be related, respectful, and reasonable. Also take the time to discuss logical consequences for the following common problems, such as someone who writes on the desk, someone who uses profanity at school, someone who doesn't do his or her work during class, or someone who is late for school. Always give children plenty of practice by working on hypothetical situations, so that there is a lack of emotional involvement and blame.

An important component to an effective approach to behavior management must ensure that behaviors learned or changed will be maintained over time and demonstrated in different contexts. The most important task with aggressive students or students with disruptive behaviors is to teach them alternatives to their angry behaviors. Tactics that are frequently implemented by teachers aware of their own impulses and that avert escalation of student anger involve the following strategies adopted from Kerr and Nelson (1998).

1. *Don't threaten.* This may be interpreted as a power play and increase fear or prompt assaultive behavior by the individual.

2. *Don't shout.* If the person with an unstable or irrational behavior seems not to be listening, it is not because he or she is hard of hearing. Other *voices* are interfering.

3. *Don't criticize.* It will only make matters worse. It cannot possibly make things better at that time.

4. *Don't squabble with other family members over best strategies or allocations of blame.* This is no time to prove a point.

5. *Don't stand over the individual if he or she is seated.* Instead, seat yourself.

6. *Avoid direct, continuous eye contact or touching the individual.* Students forced into direct eye contact may emotionally freeze or instinctively become aggressive.

Anger reactions are escape behaviors for feeling intimidated or anticipating criticism. Defensively argumentative students, for example, are only struggling to terminate conflict with the teacher and may increase volatility until the teacher ceases the contact.

SUMMARY

Most approaches to behavior management are teacher-mediated, requiring a high degree of control of self-emotions and reactions. Effective management of contingencies and direct skills instruction are two of the teacher's best tools. The complexity and intensity of working with students who exhibit behavioral challenges require high levels of dedication and expertise by professional educators and administrators. To function effectively, these persons need an adequate support system, a consistent behavior management system, and a positive approach to behavior management throughout the educational process. This chapter describes some of these approaches and suggests schoolwide and classroom approaches along with positive discipline programs. In short, teachers are responsible to design strategies for students that provide meaningful experiences and ensure retention for lifelong learning.

PEER MEDIATION AND POSITIVE DISCIPLINE WITH HARD-TO-REACH STUDENTS

Jim Ciociola

For more than 25 years, discipline has been the number one concern facing the public school systems in the United States. While most students are not discipline problems in school, others have learned over the years that in order to get attention they need to act out and cause problems. Some students cause problems for the teacher as a way of expressing their dissatisfaction with their lack of control over their surroundings. These students are accustomed to having things their own way, so when they get to school and are told what, when and how to do things, they rebel.

This chapter explores nonviolent crisis management, conflict resolution, and peer mediation as behavioral interventions for at-risk students. It also offers some tips to those who deal with the ever-growing at-risk population of students on a regular basis. There is a variety of causes for discipline problems in our schools, and several precipitating factors frequently occur. These include:

1. The loss of personal power in which the student may be trying to show that he or she is in control.

2. The maintenance of self-esteem where the student may be saving face in front of others.

3. The displacement of anger when the student acts up because of unrelated problems.

4. Failure of the student who is not able to complete simple tasks or attain the simplest of goals.

5. Frustration with a change in the normal routine.

6. Physiological and psychological reasons.

7. Current problems going on in student's neighborhood.

We now closely examine employment of schoolwide methods addressing these concerns and the empirical questions arising from their application.

COMMON FEATURES OF A SCHOOLWIDE BEHAVIOR MANAGEMENT PLAN

Total Commitment of the Staff to Manage Student Behaviors

Tim Lewis, a researcher from the University of Missouri, feels that first and foremost, faculty and staff must agree that schoolwide behavioral management is one of their priorities (Lewis, 1997). Crisis intervention, collaborative classrooms, peer mediation and conflict resolution are just some of the techniques in managing the at-risk population. Crisis intervention is a behavior management system developed to assist professionals in dealing with students who can be disruptive and, at times, assaultive. Essentially, the idea of the system is that disruptive behavior displayed is a reaction to something else, an antecedent action.

When teachers intervene to stop undesirable behavior, they must be aware that their actions have an enormous effect on how the conflict unfolds. They need to understand that, during a conflict, a series of successive actions takes place. If the teacher loses control, he or she may escalate the problem whereas remaining level-headed and offsetting the behavior with a positive response will most likely defuse the conflict. Ideally, the maximum opportunity of calming the person is to balance or neutralize the student's reactions with a therapeutic reaction.

Students who become hostile usually express their resentment in two ways: with words or actions. A typical scenario might call for the staff to use a "hands-on" approach to quiet or calm the agitated student. Unfortunately, this action might precipitate a physical confrontation that could have been avoided. If this is the case, the hands-on method has escalated the student's behavior to a more difficult and dangerous level instead of reducing it. A more appropriate staff intervention is the use of verbal intervention to safely manage the disruptive student. This technique could defuse the situation without the need for any type of physical intervention on the staff's part.

According to the National Crisis Prevention Institute (1983), there are distinct and identifiable behavior levels. By learning to identify these levels and an effective staff response, teachers can easily avert arousal of crisis situations. Sanctioned for educators is the Crisis Development Model. This model identifies four levels of crisis development and the corresponding staff responses.

The first level is anxiety. This is defined as a noticeable change in a student's normal behavior. The staff reaction should be support. This asks the teacher to be empathetic and actively listen to what is upsetting the student and to avoid becoming judgmental. Usually, a good ear can be enough to help the student in crisis.

The second level is defensive, reached when the student begins to lose rationality. Verbal and nonverbal clues or signals indicate that a person is losing control. The best staff reaction at this point is to be directive and set limits for the student. There are some key factors to setting limits. First, make sure that the limits are clear. Second, make sure that the instructions being asked are simple to understand. The student who is escalating does not need too many options thrown at him or her. The limit being imposed should be reasonable and enforceable. Teachers need to avoid mistakes of a no-win situation by issuing limits that cannot be enforced.

The acting-out person is the third definable stage. The acting-out person has reached the next behavior level, defined as total loss of control, usually resulting in aggression. At this point the staff might have to use physical restraint.

Tension reduction is the fourth and final stage of development. When students find themselves in a crisis or are trying to solve a problem, it usually results in some consequence being imposed upon them. Too often the scenario ends with the consequence. Educators forget the importance of processing the problem, offering alternatives to the student, and coming to some agreement on possible resolutions to reduce the risk of recurrence.

When dealing with students who can potentially lose control, the importance of nonverbal communication also must be addressed. Many times personal space becomes an issue. Like adults, children apparently feel safe with a "zone of comfort." Zones surround their immediate frontal area extending from one to two feet beyond arms' reach and from head to toe. Adult invasion of this comfort zone can be perceived as threatening. Usually, the student responds with a nonverbal or verbal cue of feeling uncomfortable.

Two other variables to remember are the signals that educators give others with their body and the tone of voice. Research supports (Ruben & Ruben, 1985) the idea that about 20% of any given message delivered to another person is verbal. The other 80% is interpreted from another source, that is, body language and nonverbal signals. Overuse of nonverbal communicators may sabotage classroom defusing methods and inadvertently escalate angry students. Teacher awareness of nonverbal behaviors is, assuredly, a first level of defense.

However, even methodologically astute educators can make mistakes in the heat of conflict and derail potential resolutions. Provoking students are impatient with teacher incompetence and may spot a hesitant or upset teacher. Once detected, some students may persistently antagonize, bully, or insult the confused teacher and hope he or she will explode. Inevitably, exploding in anger is desirable because *the student will then know how to interact with the teacher on his or her level.* Aggressive students who are accustomed to altercations at home or in their social lives naturally expect anger arousal in teachers as a normal part of life. Teachers who unknowingly succumb to frustration provide a level playing field on which the student, already conditioned, is an expert and can outsmart the teacher's tactics. Contrariwise, control of frustration using defusing methods not only stops altercations but removes students' familiarity and leaves them paralyzed, uncertain, and second-guessing their reactions.

Collaborative Classroom Approaches

One way around solo-teacher methodology is through collaborative classroom efforts. Collaborative classrooms are a measure that can be taken to prevent or help at-risk students from being unsuccessful. Collaborative classrooms allow students and teachers the latitude to make group decisions about the rules and limits for the class. It is extremely important for teachers to make their classrooms collaborative learning environments. Collaborative classrooms have four basic characteristics: shared knowledge among teachers and students; shared authority among teachers and students; teachers as mediators; and heterogeneous groupings of students.

One method of preventing discipline problems is to form a behavioral discipline plan that includes a collaboration among the administration, teacher, and student that could include a pro-active plan to address verbal and nonverbal disruptions. Teachers need to be aware that their actions, both verbal and nonverbal, have a direct impact on the actions of their students. Since the classroom is a microcosm of our society, students need to be involved in the development of classroom standards and guidelines. If teachers can become more aware of students' needs, they will be more effective in their instruction, thus hopefully reducing the frequency of discipline problems.

It is important for educators to be cognizant of the many precipitating factors and flexible within the classroom guidelines. Students who are highly motivated to learn are rarely the ones in trouble. Teachers should collaborate with the students to establish rules and consequences for the classroom. This list of standards and expectations should be discussed, agreed upon by all involved parties, and signed. Involving the students in making classroom decisions allows them to feel that the classroom is also theirs, and they have a vested interest in following the procedures.

One of the most often forgotten steps in dealing with disciplinary concerns is the resolution stage. This is the most important aspect of prevention, correction, and learning of appropriate behaviors. Following is listed one of many models that educators could use to problem-solve unanticipated roadblocks during implementation of programs. Quickly acting on solutions not only averts crisis but reflects teacher competence in preserving continuity of classroom strategies.

C —**Control:** Students and staff must be under control emotionally and physically.

O —**Orient:** Find out the facts of the conflict.

P —**Pattern:** Determine if there are recurrent behavior patterns within one or many students and antecedents generally prompting recurrence.

I —**Investigate:** Consider options for alleviation of behavior and restoration of program.

N —**Negotiate:** Agree to a contract, document the agreement, and have both parties sign it.

G —**Give control back to student:** Revert control back to students so they recognize they are responsible for their misbehaviors.

Peer Mediation

The implementation of peer-mediated conflict resolution is an efficient method for creating a productive school atmosphere. All students can thus develop prosocial behavior, improving the quality of teacher–student interaction by diminishing school-imposed solutions in student conflict situations.

Peer mediation is a process where students identify, negotiate, and develop solutions to school or community conflicts that interfere with learning during the normal school day. Peer mediators need to be carefully chosen and need to undergo extensive training in a structured process that requires them to become adept at active listening, reflective paraphrasing, and issues clarification within the context of the conflict at hand. Peer mediation can work very simply. Students are trained over several weeks in problem-solving techniques and approaches to conflict resolution. After the proper training, administration and staff at schools can refer conflict-oriented problems to the mediators before they become major disciplinary problems. Role of peer mediators reduces the number of office referrals and proportionally reduces student suspension rates.

Steps to Positive Exchanges with Students during Mediation or Conflict Resolution

Several documented caveats against overuse of punishment urge positive exchanges as catalysts in facilitating peer mediation. As resolvers of conflict, trained mediators act as fundamental models for other students to observe, admire, and emulate. Articulately and patiently communicated suggestions gain instant respect, personifying mediators as a powerful voice among the student body. Hostile exchanges, by contrast, interfere with verbal messages and ruin the trust originally perceived in mediators. That is why mediation training explicitly provides "dos and don'ts" to prevent altercations and swiftly resolve problems. Suggested are widely adopted guidelines to achieve this goal:

1. Avoid getting angry over the situation and be willing to express your feelings about the conflict.
2. Try to surface any hidden agenda behind the conflict by talking about, and attempting to understand, the causes.
3. Avoid the silent treatment by just walking away from the crisis.
4. Do not bring up past conflicts or negatives that have nothing to do with the current conflict.
5. Deal with the behavior, not the person.
6. Strive for a win-win situation.
7. Encourage positive statements from the disputants.
8. Listen and restate in words what the disputants said. Do not make assumptions or misquote discordant students.
9. Accept honest feedback from the other person in conflict.
10. Speak clearly and distinctly, calling the disputant by name.

IMPLEMENTATION PROBLEMS

As with any new intervention, problems invariably arise. One particularly difficult problem is teacher or student resistance to the extra work. Assuring participants that the workload decreases after implementation is one solution. However, student mediators frequently complain that interventions interfere with in-class time. Out-of-class duties may disrupt continuity of lectures and assignments, and teachers might decide to penalize either mediator or disputant for prolonged absence from the classroom.

Alternatively, flexibility is essential. "Flexibility plans" on the part of the teachers and disputants need to be agreed upon by the entire staff and student body. Teachers could reschedule some activities if a mediation or conflict dispute needs to be settled. At the same time, students assume the responsibility of using discretion. They can postpone mediation until after class when the curriculum dictates their attention, as, for example, when classes feature guest speakers.

A third problem is perceived failure of the mediation program. Success or failure may be subjective unless preliminary steps are followed to monitor mediation progress and obstacles encountered along the way. Monitoring, in part, entails weekly or monthly meetings with mediators, review and retraining of tactics, and periodic school surveys distributed to the entire student body. Attitudinal surveys, albeit general, elicit answers to basic questions such as, Do you like the mediation program, and Are mediators effective? Measurable evidence of program efficacy is not expected from attitudinal surveys, which are only a temporary yardstick of "social validity." That is, survey data present an overview of peer acceptance of the program and degree to which understanding exists of its process.

Surveys sampling student sentiment accomplish a second goal. They are instrumental in sensitizing students to nonteacher control mechanisms. Students learn their peers act as judges, jury, and critical decision makers regarding school behavior. Student problem solvers, ironically, pose a greater threat to the psychological state of students than do teachers. Mediators not only adjudicate decisions but impose opinions that instantly disseminate among all students and deeply influence their likeability and persuasive abilities to work with disputing students. Effective student mediators function as liaisons between student and teacher and earn reputations as organized peacemakers and troubleshooters rather than "troublemakers."

Survey tools sampling peer mediation effectiveness in a school vary in style and questions asked. One direct format follows a Likert-scale of rating the program by degree of agreement or disagreement. The program survey on the following page applies this method.

Class Meetings

Class meetings are procedures that create an atmosphere of self-expression and openness among students (Glasser, 1988). A class meeting is a format that strives to develop confidence as a result of stating opinions without fear to others. Class meetings involve student discussions without threat of teacher censorship or student vulnerability. There are no right or wrong answers in the interaction that takes place during the session. Everyone is strongly encouraged to participate by

James Martin Middle School
Peer Mediation Program
1998–99 Program Survey

Student Name (optional)_____

Grade Level_____

Gender_____

Race_____

Please circle the answer that best describes how you feel about each question.

SA–strongly agree; A–agree; DK–don't know; D–disagree; SD–strongly disagree

1. As a result of the mediation program our school has fewer conflicts and fights.	SA	A	DK	D	SD
2. The program has helped the school have fewer conflicts between students and teachers.	SA	A	DK	D	SD
3. I have helped others deal with a conflict this year because of what I learned in mediation.	SA	A	DK	D	SD
4. I treat people better because of what I learned in mediation.	SA	A	DK	D	SD
5. Students feel safer at James Martin since mediation was started.	SA	A	DK	D	SD
6. Teachers treat students better since the program was initiated.	SA	A	DK	D	SD
7. James Martin students accept others of different cultures, races, and genders because of mediation.	SA	A	DK	D	SD
8. The mediation program has made more students want to come to the school.	SA	A	DK	D	SD
9. Teachers like and support the peer mediation program at the school.	SA	A	DK	D	SD
10. The principal and administration like and support the peer mediation program.	SA	A	DK	D	SD
11. I feel I can handle conflicts better because of what I learned in peer mediation.	SA	A	DK	D	SD
12. Students treat each other better because of the mediation program at the school.	SA	A	DK	D	SD
13. I have a better understanding of why people act the way they do because of what was learned in the class.	SA	A	DK	D	SD
14. The mediation class has helped me think more before I make a decision to act.	SA	A	DK	D	SD
15. Peer mediation has helped me be better able to avoid fights or conflicts.	SA	A	DK	D	SD
16. The mediation program has helped me have fewer conflicts at home.	SA	A	DK	D	SD
17. The parents are aware of the peer mediation program at our school.	SA	A	DK	D	SD

expressing an opinion regarding the subject being discussed. Classroom meetings fall into three categories.

1. *Educational-diagnostic meeting.* This meeting is used to evaluate whether the students have achieved the objectives of the teaching unit. During this session, questions can be directly asked of the student to evaluate mastery of curriculum knowledge, including inquiries on homework completion and on-task efforts.

2. *Open-ended meeting.* This meeting involves a discussion of questions and issues that have no right or wrong answers. Originality of thought and creativity are encouraged. Issues may relate to the academic curriculum or the lives of the students.

3. *Problem-solving meeting.* Students discuss group and individual problems in this type of meeting. It can be used to deal with individual and group conflicts or to resolve social problems of the school itself. The atmosphere of these meetings should be positive and constructive.

Teachers interested in commencing class meetings are advised to follow a sequential format. Begin with the educational-diagnostic meetings and proceed gradually to the other two categories. Initially limiting autonomy of student input, gradually lift restrictions of student commentary until students can freely interject without retribution or perceiving themselves disruptive to the classroom meeting process. The discussion during the class meeting should be limited to the topic and possible solutions. Resolutions should be discussed thoroughly, with punishment not being the outcome. Students should remain neutral and without criticism of others. However, even structured-guided class meetings may get out of control and incapacitate teachers. A reliable method to maintain student dignity and continuity of control is to follow basic guidelines. These include:

1. Listen to the person who is speaking.
2. Do not interrupt while another person is speaking.
3. Raise hands to be recognized before speaking.
4. Stay on the topic until the topic is no longer an issue.

Initially, the teacher should facilitate the discussion during the class meeting by reviewing the purpose and guidelines for the meeting. It is important for the teacher to carefully monitor students' behavior early in the meeting to ensure the smooth flow of the meeting. Class meetings should be held at consistent times daily or at least three days a week. The length of the meeting varies. Jones and Jones (1981) suggested, for example, that the class meeting time for elementary students last between 10 and 30 minutes. Intermediate and secondary class meetings can go longer, lasting up to 30 to 45 minutes.

The major goals of class meetings are to encourage social skill development and problem-solving techniques. Increasing student responsibility for the meeting can aid in reaching these goals. After about 10 meetings, the teacher can begin to foster student control.

TIPS FOR BEHAVIORAL INTERVENTIONS

Following are basic guidelines that could be used when dealing with at-risk or escalating students. These should be considered only as an infrastructure utilized by the instructors to formulate their own teaching style and to meet any specific needs of individual students.

1. *Classroom structure and rules.* Predictability and consistency are essential to provide students the means to develop inner controls. Structure and routine convey security to students.

2. *Antiseptic bouncing.* Many times verbal and physical aggression can be avoided by providing the student an escape from the conflict or problem. This can be done in the form of delivering messages to the office or borrowing something from another teacher. The hope is that by the time the student has been bounced to a different situation and returns to the crisis, that student has ceased to be angry and is amenable to resolutions.

3. *Humor.* Overuse of any anecdotal methods can be ineffective. Humor is a good example. Used correctly, humor can be a powerful intervention, especially in defusing potential volatile situations. Joking with the student at times does not supplant an adult's authority.

4. *Signal interference.* As stated previously, nonverbal communications are very powerful. Let the student know that the behavior is not acceptable through eye contact, hand gestures, or body posture.

5. *Restructuring.* This procedure involves modifying the class situation so that conflicts are less likely to materialize. Any variation in activities might make a difference and bring about more fitting academic and social behavior.

6. *Reality appraisal.* Explain to students why a behavior is unacceptable. This assists students in understanding any positive or negative consequences of the behavior, allowing students to take responsibility for the behavior.

PREVENTION OF BEHAVIOR PROBLEMS USING ACADEMICS

Often students' behavior problems can be traced to problems in instructional design and implementation. By incorporating general principles of positive academic programming, many problems can be prevented. When designing an academic program, the teacher should consider the following questions:

1. Will the student understand the goals of the academic program?
2. Will the student know that the work is leading to something meaningful?
3. Have there been clear expectations established for participation?
4. Are there precise and explicit instructions in simple and understandable terms?
5. Will instructional activities be planned in advance?
6. Does the instructional planning reflect a predictable structure in which there can be student participation?
7. Are subjects ready to be taught as soon as the students enter the class?

8. Is there a variety of instructional presentation strategies planned (group work, special projects, student presentations)?

9. Is the academic setting positive?

10. Is the classroom a fun place to learn?

11. Is the class safe and orderly?

12. Do the students know where to pick up and return work?

13. Is minimal class time spent on record keeping?

14. Are the rules posted and visible?

15. Are there class rules?

16. Do the rules specify observable behaviors?

17. Are the rules positive?

18. Are they reasonable and enforceable?

19. Are they concise?

20. Have the rules been discussed and agreed upon by the class?

21. Is there a system for addressing instructional and behavioral problems?

22. Have problems in academics and behavior been anticipated?

23. Is problem solving pro-active or reactive?

24. When a problem arises, are choices for resolution provided?

SUMMARY

Briefly overviewed are classroom methods and solutions typically found in peer mediation and classroom meeting systems. While methods are reasonably simple to implement, caution is particularly noteworthy for high-risk students unaccustomed to structured classrooms or dealing with their peers in formal dyadics. Temptation for classroom disturbance is high, and unanticipated disturbances can deflect teachers from primary goals of behavior resolution. The obstacles, in other words, not the methodology, present the greatest challenge for educators. Control over students, like control over classrooms, thus lies in two basic strategies.

First is remembering that high-risk, volatile students significantly act out under unstructured environments. Even minimal structure mitigates their fury. Second, at-risk students channeled into problem-solving modes such as with peer mediation may resist due to feeling intimidated or inexperienced. They may have interpersonal deficits impairing communication and fostering distrust. Patience with these deficiencies and anticipation of their derailing potential can avert failures in classroom programs.

8

Community-Based Instruction and Experiences in Building Self-Esteem

Suzanne S. Piazzola

One does not have to be a professional in the field of education to realize that there are problems in our nation's schools. One merely has to pick up a newspaper or turn on the television to know something is wrong. Usually, when people talk about problems in education, they are referring to large, urban school systems, which face unique challenges in educating a student body that is disproportionately from low-income families (Hodges & Webb, 1996). Problems in big-city schools are more numerous, costly, and difficult to solve. One of the greatest problems facing these schools is discipline (Stephens, 1995).

Educators view safety in schools and disruptive behaviors as the most pressing issues facing them today (Elam et al., 1996). Teaching and learning are hampered by students' disrespect for authority, apathy, violence, and disruptive class behaviors, factors that are compounded by a lack of parental support and community involvement. This chapter presents philosophies and suggestions about the educational needs of one of the most challenging groups of students in public education. The recommendations are based on statistics regarding outcomes of at-risk youth, professional literature related to instructional and behavioral interventions, and 16 years' experience in the public school system.

CURRENT CONCERNS AND ISSUES

Growing public concern is being expressed about the future of our nation's schools and the quality of twenty-first-century employees, neighbors, and taxpayers, a large number of whom will be drawn from urban schools. These schools, usually with limited resources, serve the largest numbers of students from low-income families who are often in need of extensive remedial assistance. There is an achievement gap between the performance of students who attend big-city schools that serve poor students and their counterparts in upperclass suburban and rural schools (Hodges & Webb, 1966). The longer the students stay in school, the wider the gap becomes (Olson & Jerald, 1998). A strong possibility is that these students will drop out before they have any skills to support themselves (Walker et al., 1995). Failure of schools to prepare these students to become self-supporting, contributing members of the community has a negative effect on their quality of life and on the entire social and economic system (Siegel et al., 1990). What is at stake here is "America's future, nothing short of that."

Paul T. Hill, director of the Center for Reinventing Public Education at the University of Washington, is quoted as saying that he "doesn't think any of the large cities have a 'grip at all' on how to make the schools better" (Hodges & Webb, 1996). Robert S. Peterkin of Harvard University's Urban Superintendents' Program states that there is still a great deal of uncertainty as to whether large systems can deliver (Hodges & Webb, 1996). This comment is typical of the barrage of criticism about education in our nation's public schools. It is usually followed by a list of reform goals to be achieved, but there is little critical analysis of the factors related to problems in education or ways to change the system. Although the clock is ticking, and the public's money and patience are running out, solutions to problems in schools do exist (Hodges & Webb, 1996).

Commitment: Precursor to Change

Before reform can take place, educators must realize the impact they have on a student's success or failure in school. It has been recommended that to prevent, manage, and replace behaviors that are reducing the effectiveness of schools, alternative approaches should be implemented (Goldstein, 1994). The current education system is often unsuccessful because the traditional curriculum and teaching methods are not appropriate for all students. It is no surprise that students become bored, frustrated, and aggressive, demonstrate behavior problems, and drop out of school when they do not "fit" a system that they find boring and irrelevant. Reports on violence, aggressive behavior, dropout rates, teacher frustration, and public dissatisfaction with education demand an increase in efforts to change a system that is failing (Elam et al., 1996). Measures and strategies that are needed to achieve success under extraordinary circumstances must be examined (Hodges & Webb,1996).

The Urban Superintendents' Association of America supports the belief that American schools can produce citizens who will make a difference in creating a positive future for our nation. The goal of the association is to stimulate and support efforts to get students interested in learning and to open windows to visionary ideas and concepts in urban education. Better educating at-risk students requires the long-term, concerted efforts of many people: parents, principals, teachers, politicians, community groups, public agencies, businesses, and religious leaders.

Need to Provide Alternative Approaches to Education

Recent studies have indicated that the interventions that are most effective in correcting problem behaviors are academic and curricular restructuring, social skills training, and behavioral interventions. Research findings suggest that an instructional approach to problem behaviors is more effective than a punitive approach. Punishment often has no effect upon problem behaviors and may even serve to escalate negative behaviors (Lewis, 1997).

Teachers who have worked with inner-city students with behavior problems have observed that students who are in classes in which they feel confident about their abilities exhibit fewer aggressive behaviors and are more motivated (Myles & Simpson, 1994). They suggest that a fundamental way to decrease behavior problems is to increase motivation and feelings of self-worth by emphasizing students' abilities and interests. Teachers have excellent opportunities to observe and form opinions about educating students. As an educator in the public school system for the past 16 years, this author will share a couple of experiences that support implementing alternative approaches to meet the needs of students who exhibit problem behaviors and who are at risk of dropping out of school before they graduate. When this author began her teaching career, she was among the underprepared teachers referred to by Olson and Jerald (1998) as being disproportionately assigned to schools with limited resources (usually large, urban school districts). Statistically speaking, this author may have been part of the problem; students this author was inexperienced to work with were unmotivated, aggressive, volatile, and, in some cases, dangerous. According to the professional literature on at-risk students, they fitted the pattern of chronic discipline problems and truancy. They committed crimes and got arrested (Walker et al., 1995). They also followed the pattern of dropping out of school to commit crimes full-time (Office of Juvenile Justice and Delinquency Prevention [OJJDP], 1995).

While this author was busy teaching the prescribed curriculum, they were concerned about such matters as where their next meal would come from or whether they were pregnant. Students were worried about violence and threats to their safety. It was difficult to compete under these circumstances; what difference did it make where the comma went? The police were such frequent visitors to the school and to my classroom that this author jokingly suggested that they build a precinct on campus to conserve time and energy (today, they have one directly across the street from the school). The potentially violent nature of some students did not impact this author until the morning paper featured a picture of one of this author's students on the front page. He was shown lying face down on the sidewalk, surrounded by police and spectators; he had been shot in the back by a sixth grader because he "bullied" her. The previous morning he had been sitting in my classroom writing a journal about his future plans. This author had been taught about how to make bulletin boards, not how to send home a student's last written words to his grieving parents.

Student fights occurred on a daily (and sometimes hourly) basis. Teachers were threatened and, occasionally, assaulted by students. Student behaviors, although typical of difficult students (Canter & Canter, 1993), interfered with teaching and learning: they disrupted class constantly, were unmotivated, did not complete assigned work, and confronted authority. To these students, most of whom were from a poor socioeconomic area, the curriculum had no apparent relevance whatsoever to their lives or future. Their behavior problems were a result of disinterest and boredom and, less commonly, an inability to do the work. The mandated curriculum included course work, strategies, and materials related to higher scores on standardized tests and successful academic performance. It did not consider the unique problems that prevented at-risk students from progressing in school. Grades and standardized test scores are insufficient motivators of many at-risk students. These students need experiences that are relevant, interesting, and important enough to prepare them for the future and prevent them from dropping out of school.

Although this teacher survived that first year of teaching at-risk students, it was out of determination to let the students know that they could depend on someone. This author showed them respect and gained theirs. Although I did not realize it at the time, the author's teaching style was what the literature describes as a therapeutic teaching style (Myles & Simpson, 1994). At the expense of earning "perfect attendance," this author suffered from the stress often associated with teaching aggressive students (Curwin & Mendler, 1988).

In fact, this author was seriously contemplating a career switch when she received a call from the public defender to speak on behalf of one of her students. His mother had requested this author based on the rapport established with this student.

An extremely at-risk student, his reading level was several grades below his placement (probably because he was absent more than he was in school). Family problems and responsibilities kept him out of school frequently. His behaviors made him difficult to tolerate when he was in school; he had failing grades, and he was involved in the wrong things outside school. In one of his journal entries he had written that he wanted to make something of himself and not "wind up like his uncle." He said he was going to come to school every day and try harder. But he was no longer in school, and now the school had "one less problem to deal with."

In this instance, the school may not have been able to compete with the student's environment, but when he left the system, he did not cease to be a problem. Every day the system fails students like him. Since then this author changed schools several times, but the students' problems were basically the same. One student in particular convinced this author she needed to work harder to bring about changes for at-risk students. According to academic standards, he was not a "good" student. He made straight Fs, was tardy to all of his classes, cut school, and was always "in trouble" with teachers and administrators, who treated him as though he did not have a single redeeming factor.

When he finally studied and passed a science test, the teacher accused him of cheating. He liked to draw, so this author asked him to draw a picture of an Indian woman from a magazine. Without saying a word, he gathered together scotch tape and typing paper and returned to his seat. Several days later he handed the author a poster-sized picture of the Indian woman. He had brought her to "life." Truly the creation of someone with great talent, she was perfectly shaded and detailed with her eyes closed and her face turned upward toward the sky as if in prayer. This student's drawing still hangs on my wall and tears at this author's heart, for he dropped out of school in the 10th grade. His so-called education comprised low-expectations, failing grades, negative feedback, and disciplinary actions. He walks the streets, unemployed and on drugs, his talent and future wasted.

Need for Alternative Approaches

The result of this author's boot-camp experiences in urban settings strongly urged the application of alternative programs for those students who were not academically inclined, who were at risk of dropping out, and who were unsuccessful in traditional academic programs. These students needed to prepare for a job while they were still in school. They would benefit from a more functional academic curriculum and from hands-on training and job experience. Educators need to consider the programs that more appropriately meet the specific and diverse needs of at-risk students. Altered curricula prevent students from potential risks as "dropouts." Dropout rates predictably lead to and impact the downward trend of education in general (Conley & Noble, 1990).

Purpose of Alternative Programs

Alternative programs should provide a more relevant education to those students whose lack of interest or ability prevents them from making satisfactory progress in the traditional academic setting. It is important to identify potential dropouts and place them in an alternative program because of the disproportionately large numbers of at-risk students who drop out of school before they can receive the benefits of job training (Finn, 1989). Involving students in meaningful, goal-directed experiences provides them with a reason to finish school. The purpose of the alternative curriculum is to develop students' competence and feelings of self-worth in order to increase their opportunities in the community, change community perception, and encourage increased opportunities for employment in the community. In order to promote more successful outcomes for students, it is important to design programs that:

1. Incorporate career exploration and education into the curriculum.
2. Assess career interests, aptitudes, and job skills.
3. Incorporate vocational and career planning into the curriculum.
4. Form a link between teacher engagement and student achievement (Lewis, 1997).
5. Develop a collaborative culture that promotes renewal of curricular and instructional methods.
6. Teach students functional, community-referenced, and job-related skills and provide opportunities for students to generalize skills learned in school to integrated community settings (Moore et al., 1990).
7. Encourage personnel to implement approaches that enhance students' personal choice and self-determination (Halpern, 1990).

8. Foster empowerment, ownership, and responsibility that lead to personal growth and individual competence (Wehman, 1990).

9. Strengthen the connection between school and the community it serves (OJJDP, 1995).

10. Include procedures to measure progress and ensure project and participant accountability and to determine whether to modify future programs to ensure improved student outcomes (Rojewski, 1992).

11. Develop ways of enhancing students' personal choice and self-determination (Halpern, 1990).

12. Help students realize the purpose of learning and enable them to generalize the skills they learn.

Career Exploration and Education

One of the key recommendations to improving student behaviors is to provide activities that are interesting to students and in which they have some abilities (Clarke et al., 1995). A vital part of the process of exploring interests and abilities is career counseling. The complexity of today's market requires students to be exposed to career education, vocational education, and career development, in order to provide them with an opportunity to identify careers to which they can match their skills, talents, and interests. Career education is infused into the alternative diploma curriculum in order to expose students to a full range of careers. Because of low expectations of vocational and career prospects and immature perceptions of basic job requirements, these students may have a limited awareness of careers from which to choose. Students who are informed about various careers are more capable of identifying career preferences (McLoughlin & Lewis, 1990).

Assessment of Students' Interests and Abilities

Studies involving adolescents at the secondary level indicate that specific vocational assessment needs include:

1. An assessment model that is student-centered and sensitive to developmental growth.

2. Assessment results that can be applied to programming and instruction.

3. Relationship to current and local job markets and to vocational programs offered.

4. Conduct by professionals who are trained to conduct vocational assessment (Wehby, 1994).

Systematic vocational assessment and evaluation are precursors to program involvement (Rojewski, 1992). Assessment must provide a comprehensive overview of students' vocational and career knowledge, interests and abilities, and social skills. A vital part of career and vocational assessment is determining the knowledge and awareness students have about careers and jobs. Assessment of entry-level vocational skills is also a precursor to planning vocational programs. It is important to consider the school, home, and community when assessing and programming students for careers. There are numerous competence and criterion-referenced tests available for use in initial and ongoing assessment. Caution should be taken when selecting commercially prepared assessment packages for use in planning a meaningful program for students because they may be biased and unrelated to the student's curriculum. Sometimes, work or job samples may be more appropriate than commercially prepared assessment instruments (McLoughlin & Lewis, 1990). Regardless of the method of assessment, students' strengths and interests need to be identified and matched to job situations.

Program Planning

In order to facilitate development of these competencies, students should be involved in planning their programs. Beginning with the students' entrance to high school, their backgrounds and interests should be reviewed and incorporated to make the curriculum relevant and rewarding. The process of allowing students to help develop their programs improves the chances of students' reaching their goals. It helps them assume ownership of their programs and develop a better understanding of its purpose. The plan should be reviewed with the students periodically as they progress through the program. An appropriately developed curriculum plan acts as a coordinating mechanism throughout the program and helps fulfill the outline for completing the program requirements.

Parents are also encouraged to participate in the planning of students' programs in order that they may be informed about various options available and help their children explore appropriate career interests. Parents are significant partners in the process because the aspirations they have for their children greatly influence their educational and vocational values (Wehman, 1990).

Counseling

Programs for at-risk students should also offer counseling or self-help groups to help students develop self-esteem and improve social skills (Patterson et al., 1992). Counseling or self-help groups can increase the success of at-risk individuals by helping students develop a stronger sense of their assets and limitations, awareness about the effect of their learning in the classroom and on the job, and compensation skills to help them deal with problems. Poor social skills, lack of self-discipline, and limited coping skills can cause students to experience negative outcomes both in the workforce and in the community. They have difficulty keeping jobs and they become more dependent on families, less satisfied with themselves and their lives, less involved in social relationships, and more frustrated and depressed. Counseling can also address self-determination skills, which have been recognized by researchers as a component that must be introduced into students' curriculum. Self-determination includes behaviors such as assertiveness, self-advocacy, creativity, and independence. Students who have received direct instruction in self-determination skills have demonstrated the ability to acquire, maintain, and generalize skills that focus on self-advocacy and self-awareness, which are currently considered to be particularly helpful to at-risk students. They found ways to generalize strategies they personally developed in school to the workplace and community (Ward, 1988).

Vocational and Job-Related Skill Training

Many students who are not provided access to appropriate vocational preparation complete school with no employable skills (Rosenthal, 1989). Once students' academic and technical skills are matched to a changing spectrum of careers, numerous training methods appear to be successful; they include cooperative vocational education, individual and work-crew job coaching, on-the-job training, structured job tryouts, and competitive employment. Extensive vocational skills training is vital to students who plan to move directly from high school to employment. All programs should seek to build appropriate work habits and develop work histories before students exit high school (Rojewski, 1992).

Responsible vocational training agencies should coordinate plans and guidelines. Specific vocational training is vital, but the nature of employment suggests that students need to be able to adapt to changes in work demands and to be able to acquire new skills. Effective vocational program components focus on attitudes, values, and marketable skills students need to become self-sufficient individuals (D'Alonzo et al., 1988). In addition to teaching specific vocational skills, vocational training should also address the need for students be able to adapt to changes in work demands.

Community-Based "Classrooms"

While vocational training improves chances of becoming employed initially, job retention and advancement may depend on certain types of academic competencies. A more functional approach is recommended as an alternative to educating students at risk. Providing community-based instruction allows students to become actively engaged in learning and practicing key functional skills needed for success within natural community environments. An alternative curriculum that shifts to a more relevant, interesting orientation helps decrease apathy and restlessness and allows students to gain confidence as they directly apply basic skills in the community. When they are involved and are successful, their self-confidence increases, and their behavior problems decrease (Clarke et al., 1995).

Community Support

Developing a variety of community connections and services is vital to the development of employable skills (Rojewski, 1992). Community contacts are needed for job placement opportunities, transportation, financial planning, and resource and agency referrals. Business partnerships with schools are needed to help prepare students to be contributing members of the community when they leave school. Individuals who experience difficulty in the community often require additional assistance and training in order to be successful. Collaboration must be established between schools and potential employers in order to design programs that meet the needs of businesses in the community and develop the employable skills of students.

Personnel Preparation

It has been suggested that one of the problems affecting large public school systems is that underprepared teachers are disproportionately assigned to schools that serve the largest numbers of students from low-income families (usually the case in urban school systems) and who are often in need of extensive remediation and support (Olson & Jerald, 1998). To better prepare personnel to work with at-risk students, teacher training methods and goals must be based on complete understanding of the roles and functions for which they must be trained and training approaches that are effective in this area. If teachers react to students' aggressive behaviors with fear, avoidance, and counteraggression, the students' behaviors are likely to escalate and become more frequent (Swick, 1987). In order to maintain a positive relationship with at-risk students, educators must be able to respect their students and help the students manage their stress (Myles & Simpson, 1994).

Curriculum modifications should be made in the preservice programs of future professionals in order to increase awareness and understanding of the manifestations and needs of students who display aggressive behaviors or are discipline problems in school. For instance, Good and Brophy (1990) describe effective teachers as those who are enthusiastic about teaching, have cheerful attitudes, are generally liked by their students, and expect positive things from themselves and their students. They are able to manage stress in a number of ways and provide a positive classroom in which students are able to succeed (Swick, 1987).

Job-Seeking and Placement

Another component of the alternative curriculum includes structured job-seeking opportunities to help students develop skills required to seek and obtain employment. Job-seeking activities are résumé writing, completing job applications, practicing job interviews, locating job prospects, and contacting potential employers. Students' abilities and interests are considered relative to supported employment options (Rojewski, 1992).

Coping Skills and Problem-Solving Skills

Students can become more successful by developing coping strategies. Although many of these strategies are learned through trial and error, specific coping skills can be taught. The curriculum must include instruction in compensation skills and generalization of knowledge to work situations. It is vital for students to possess coping skills to help them meet the demands of the workplace and community. Students need to be equipped with a "spectrum of general problem-solving strategies" as well as basic skills (Rojewski, 1992). By providing instruction that links academic problem solving to vocational problem solving, educators can help students to see that they can employ the same strategies to solve both academic and vocational tasks.

Follow Up/Follow Along

The process of ongoing assessment of students' performance is necessary to determine effectiveness of programs and improve the outcome of individuals exiting our nation's schools. Follow-up services should include identification of variables to be examined and ways to collect information that can be used to guide program development for at-risk youth. Halpern (1990) suggests that programs include attention to factors that affect students' quality of life: the degree to which they have control over their environment and the ability they have to sustain a viable self in the social world.

MODEL PROGRAMS

Although there are no model urban schools to follow in developing programs (Olson & Jerald, 1998), a number of model programs are described in the literature as leading to the improvement of outcomes of students with special needs who are at risk of failing or dropping out of school. These models focus primarily on preparing students for the world of work and community living. The model programs include components that focus on student involvement in relevant, hands-on experiences that are based on an assessment of students' job interests and abilities. They provide at-risk students with a meaningful, goal-directed curriculum fosters self-worth and decreases disruptive, nonproductive behaviors and leads to successful outcomes of students exiting our nation's public schools.

Model Program 1

One innovative approach places individuals into entry-level, competitive employment (Wehman, 1990). Phase 1 is conducted over a six-month period and involves utilization of assessment data and development of an employment success plan. An eight-week training period is spent on employable skills such as job-seeking skills, self-awareness, adjustment skills, communication, decision making, job tryouts, and supported job searches. Phase 2 involves direct job placement, support/follow-up as needed, and ongoing support through job club meetings. Phase 3 involves job change/job advancement services. The key components of the Job Training and Tryout Model are:

- Assessment and evaluation
- Employment success planning

- Employable skills training
- Job tryouts for which students receive a training stipend
- Weekly work adjustment seminars
- Supported job searches and job placement
- Six-month follow-up and support
- Job club for ongoing support
- Job change and advancement assistance

Model Program 2

D'Alonzo et al. (1988) created project MEAL (Model for Employment and Adult Living), a life skills training program designed to move unemployed youth to successful employment and community living. Initial screening and preliminary assessment were followed by job-specific training. An eight-week program provided independent living skills training, job readiness skills, academic tutoring, and work experience. Job placement was included in the program.

Key components of project MEAL are:

- Diagnosis and assessment
- Academic and vocational training based on assessment and goals
- Training program that includes developing job-related attitudes and behaviors, job training and placement, and independent living skills
- Financial planning

Model Program 3

Rojewski (1992) describes a four-phase process designed to assist high school students prepare for the transition to adult life. Phase 1 was initiated in 9th or 10th grade and involved assessment and evaluation of student needs. Phase 2 involved work adjustment training, academic support, independent living, and job-seeking skills. Phase 3 consisted of planning for future school years and preparation for postsecondary activities. Phase 4 consisted of actual transition, involving job search/placement. Model components included:

- Assessment and evaluation
- Vocational counseling
- Vocational exploration and training
- Academic support
- Personal growth groups that focused on social skills training
- Collaboration with industry and businesses
- Job placement and job modification

Model Program 4

Rosenthal (1989) proposed a three-year, high school-based program, Project JOB. Year 1 activities included multidimensional vocational assessment and exploration. Year 2 involved experience-based education, which consisted of internships, guest speakers, and field visits. Year 3 focused on job-seeking activities and job placement. Key components of the program included:

- Assessment and evaluation
- Experience-based career education with exploratory activities
- Job training through internships
- Raising of students' expectations through counseling—both vocational and personal/social
- Job placement and follow-up

Model Program 5

The Career Ladder Program (CLP), designed for the placement and training of high school seniors to help them make the transition from school to adult life (Siegal et al., 1990), provides a half day for monitored work experience in a real work-setting community classroom. Criteria for vocational and social objectives are established, and an employment skills workshop is held once a week in which students learn entry-level job skills, social skills, peer counseling techniques, and job search skills. Key components of the CLP were:

- Follow-up contact on a quarterly basis
- On-the-job training—task analysis and job coaching
- Independent living skills—financial matters, apartment finding, obtaining a driver's license
- Counseling
- Social skills training
- Ecosystematic intervention
- Job search counseling (job-seeking skills, training to job placement)

Model Program 6

Rosenthal's (1989) transition project, CAREER, was a transition program designed specifically to facilitate career-job training through experience-based education. Goals included exposing students to career options, job settings, and career orientations through experience-based internships; providing opportunities to gain work-transferable personal and vocational skills and information; and assisting in meeting academic and job demands through computer-assisted writing and compensatory strategies. Key components of CAREER included:

- Assessment and evaluation
- Experience-based career education
- Job training through internships
- Counseling
- Job placement and follow-up

Model Program 7

The Competitive Employment through Vocational Experiences (CETVE) model (Test et al., 1988) was a process designed to provide competitive and volunteer work experiences for secondary-level students to allow them to develop a work history before they graduate. The three phases of CETVE included identification of students who needed CETVE services; screening to identify employment skills; placing students in competitive or volunteer work situations; and training conducted by a job coach. Also part of the program, follow-along services were provided to ensure job retention. The key components of CETVE were:

- Referrals based on employment training needs
- Review of evaluation data and student interviews
- On-the-job training and advocacy through the job coach
- Job placement in competitive employment
- Follow-along services
- Collaboration with business and industry

Building Success through Relevant Experiences

Not all of the models have the same components, but there are commonalities shared by each of the model programs. The alternative program the author currently implements has a specific, sequential curriculum that is designed to provide students with the knowledge, skills, and job-related behaviors they need to enter work and community successfully. "Employability training," the focus of this alternative program, addresses academics, career preparation, job-related training, and job experience. Each of the courses is related to students' future plans and career interests, and each area of skill is directly applicable to work or community.

For instance, functional academics replaces traditional English requirements with practical activities such as reading bus schedules and maps, ordering from catalogs, writing memos and letters of complaint, filling out forms, balancing checkbooks, personal budgets, and so on. Instead of students' reading Beowulf and writing research papers, typically part of the curriculum for college-bound students, students read technical manuals, recipes, newspapers, schedules, and driver's manuals. Curriculum-based experiences are crucial components of the learning experience. For instance, students first read a bus schedule in the classroom. Then they travel by bus to various destinations in the community, such as banks, shopping malls, restaurants, post offices, or other community "classrooms." Students go into stores and determine how much their budgets will allow them to spend or how much sales save them. They place orders from menus and determine how much to tip. They learn how to open bank accounts or checking accounts, apply for loans, register for selective service.

The implementation of curriculum-based instruction as a follow-up to classroom instruction is an effective approach to making school relevant. It helps students become actively involved in learning and helps them to be more successful by allowing them to apply the skills they learn in the classroom in the "real world." Providing situations that allow students to practice problem solving in the community helps to equip students with a spectrum of general problem-solving strategies.

The job prep component of the program consists of a hands-on assessment of students' vocational interests and aptitudes. Students "rotate" through a series of vocational classes over a period of six months before they are placed in a specific vocational area. Students are not expected to choose a vocation without prior knowledge or experience. Surprising results have occurred through this process, such as having a female student choose welding for her vocational class placement. Opposed to even trying welding at first, she completed the course and became certified in welding. Other students have seen the success of students who have completed the program, and they are becoming motivated and cooperative and are working to reach their goals.

The program allows students to demonstrate acquired employable skills through school-based jobs and community experiences. Successful completion of job-skill development leads to placement in jobs in the community for which they receive pay and earn credits toward a diploma. Throughout their course of study, students develop a portfolio that includes a transcript of job competencies; course work; job-related skills; job experiences at school and in the community; and recommendations from teachers, supervisors, and employers.

This program has been the best approach to changing problem behaviors that the author has used in 16 years of teaching. Positive changes in students have been evident throughout the school. There have been fewer discipline notes, better attitudes and cooperation, and fewer confrontations with administrators and teachers because students are now driven by purposeful goals and high expectations.

Noteworthy is one final and very different scenario about how schools can affect student behaviors. Early this year two of the most problematic students in school were placed in the alternative program. After several months of involvement in the program, they made a video about their program to show the faculty. They filmed students at work in vocational activities, school jobs, and community-based activities. They stood in front of the faculty and explained the video with such pride that everyone knew a great transformation had taken place and that these students had a much brighter future. Other students in the program were there also—to serve the faculty refreshments they had made themselves.

CONCLUSION

As predicted in the literature, students who are actively participating in the learning process are less likely to be frustrated and aggressive, and their disruptive behaviors decrease (Clarke et al., 1995). Such was the case with the students described in the previous section. As a result of the improved behaviors of these students, the faculty has begun to change their attitudes toward them. Teachers' perceptions and expectations of them are helping students to feel better about themselves and to improve further. Teachers report less stress because their efforts to teach are more productive, and they deal less with behavior problems.

The success of these programs demonstrate that educators can engage in certain tactics that eliminate problem behaviors. The implication of studies is that regardless of whether an alternative program is implemented or if components of the alternative curriculum are utilized, innovative curricular and instructional behavioral approaches should be examined as a way to address problems in education and improve the outcomes of students exiting our public school system.

9

Teaching Students with Serious Emotional and Behavioral Problems: A Teacher's Perspective

Barry G. Macciomei

Teaching, advising, and socializing with students who exhibit maladaptive behaviors and emotional disorders can be rewarding. However, most educators and administrators don't think this is true, due to the lack of knowledge and the mishandling of daily problems and confrontations. Successful work with difficult students is no picnic. To work successfully with these students, whether on elementary or secondary levels, it is important to recognize the type of individual you are dealing with. Staying "objective" is the necessity of survival. The teacher or principal must always remember an important rule of thumb: *the student* is the seriously disturbed person who may be out of control, not *the teacher*. Consequently, *never* allow yourself to be brought down to their these students' of thinking or reacting.

Put in straightforward terms: *never allow the students' behaviors to control the teachers' behaviors.* Throughout this chapter, practical concepts for altering behaviors are discussed as well as various cases illustrated, all addressing the proverbial question, How do you really control seriously disturbed and disruptive students? Briefly introduced are basic tenets followed in using any approach despite your background or orientation. Second, actual experiences are reviewed demonstrating not only applications of technique but peculiar and untoward repercussions encountered that required secondary and tertiary techniques.

THE LAW OF SURVIVAL: CHANGE BEHAVIOR, THEN TEACH

Unpopular as it may seem, the first premise you must make is that behavior must be altered before you can successfully implement classroom instruction. This, unfortunately, is not the case throughout the public school systems. Consequently, there are serious teacher–student or student–student conflicts all day long. The large-scale outcomes are that instruction rarely occurs within classrooms of disturbed students and is reflected by these students' scoring low on standardized, end-of-year state tests. Purely focusing on curriculum overlooks the disputing students' lack of learning readiness and creates unrealistic and unachievable lesson goals. Even curriculum-minded teachers intent on pushing lessons must face the obvious: skill learning occurs only when teachers reward positive behavior and punish negative behavior (Walker & Seerson, 1990). Through this consistent process, one can begin to alter behavior enough to begin to educate.

Long and Morse (1996) concur that the three major areas of focus in altering behaviors are consistency, success, and movement. Let us examine each area relative to my own classroom environment.

Consistency

All school systems have some degree of behavior problems. However, many schools have a higher proportion of students with oppositional, explosive, or disruptive behaviors. Choice of disciplinary program and classroom technique may vary by school and teacher preference. Typically, in fact, choice of technique is like pieces of chalk. You keep using it until it runs down or loses its potency. Eclectically selecting methods based on its rapid effectiveness or even user-friendly strategy inherently poses many problems. But the worst problem is inconsistency. The teacher or administrator must implement programs for a period of time for students to receive all consequences promised. Consistency not only means "doing it the same way each time but also clarifying the method and consequences."

Succinctly explained methods and consequences allow the student to immediately understand behavior contingencies and adequately make efforts to comply with dignity. A third problem with consistency is multiple chiefs in a tribe. Frequently, there are several school authority figures implementing the strategy or variations of the strategy who deviate from definitions and consequence-delivery methods according to their personal preference. Altered procedures may seem unimportant to implementers and, in fact, differences may be so subtle that authority figures may believe they are using the exact, defined methods. But deviations of any size are conspicuous; students with serious behavior problems clearly detect procedural discrepancy and manipulate the situation to their advantage.

Success

Creating a successful educational environment is crucial. Success means employing intrinsic and extrinsic motivation in daily lesson plans and in classroom routines. This is so important because academic failure is usually expected with this type of student and often has becomes a self-fulfilling prophecy by secondary school. Emotionally disturbed students face repeated failures, grow immune to getting in trouble, and largely believe learning is futile. By contrast, integrative steps at building success mean three things. First is having a behavioral plan that starts where the students' skills are. Second is setting realistic expectations that are immediately attainable by some or all of the students. Third is proportionally focusing more on positive, rather than negative, emotional changes in the classroom.

Movement

Movement may be the most difficult strategy to create in a school or classroom. This can be accomplished by multiage grouping, mainstreaming students in electives as well as academic classes. Lack of movement or restricting autonomy earnable by students is also effective. Movement or lack of movement can easily be enforced based on consequences and rewards for specific behaviors. Many interventions can be utilized such as level systems, point systems, token economy systems, and a minor consequence system using contracts or daily behavior sheets. Movement, confinement, or even frequent shifting functions as reinforcer for two reasons. First is that it removes students from sheltered or restricted resource rooms apart from peers. Lifting this limited access provides socialization and discounts their image of being in a special education service. Second, movement acts as a reward as a progressive step to level of "trustee." That is, deserving students realize they are steps ahead of being permanently confined to resource rooms and may remain mainstreamed provided their classroom behaviors are appropriate.

CASE ILLUSTRATIONS

Effectively implementing strategy depends on properly using consistent measures at the outset of behavior problems. Consistency, especially, creates a regimen and incentive system for many acting-out students to identify with and figure they may "win at." Perceived manipulation of a system may bolster student motivation, despite realizing later their efforts to beat the system actually will produce desirable outcomes. In the following case, Tony, a hostile juvenile, discovers his street-smart acumen may work to his advantage in meeting criteria for a classroom program.

Case of Tony: Taming Passive-Aggressive Behavior

Tony, a streetwise, acting-out, aggressive 15-year-old, was constantly in the office for behavior problems. If he wasn't fighting, he was cursing, oppositional, and defiant to authority figures. When brought to the office, Tony would not have direct eye contact and would not speak. Quite frankly, it was amusing to watch Tony manipulate the administrators with his passive-aggressive techniques. The principal would tell Tony what he did wrong while Tony stared at the floor or ceiling. Tony would not give any response to what the principal was saying. The more the administrator tried to get his point across, the angrier and more frustrated he became.

As Tony remained quiet and noncommunicative, the principal became slightly out of control, raising his voice, demanding that Tony look at him and respond. In a short time, Tony had manipulated the situation without saying a word and totally controlled the principal's emotions and eventual outcome—suspension.

Later that day, in private, I told the principal about Tony. I explained that Tony's passive-aggressive behaviors could be altered and even reversed by giving control back to the authority figures. A plan was made with the principal that the next time Tony was brought to the office, there would be no dialogue until eye contact was made. Tony would have to sit, facing the wall, for as long as it took. An explanation would be given to Tony that he would have to look at the principal when he was speaking to him.

Later that week, Tony again appeared in the office for similar oppositional and defiant behaviors. The principal initiated a conversation but saw that Tony refused to look at him. He stopped talking and told Tony to face the wall, sitting in the corner. The principal told Tony that he could not speak until the principal was ready to talk to him again. Ten minutes passed, and the principal asked Tony if he was ready to look and respond appropriately to what the principal had to say. Tony made no response. The principal then calmly responded that he will stay in that corner until the principal was ready to speak to him.

Fifteen minutes passed and the principal again asked Tony if he was ready to look and respond to the principal. Tony only looked at the ceiling. The principal did not speak, turned his back, and began working on other important matters. After 30 more minutes, Tony made one more attempt to control the situation by stating that he would listen. The principal started to talk to him, but Tony then stared at the floor. The principal stated that he would not talk to him until he maintained eye contact and told Tony to get back in the corner.

The principal let Tony sit there for one hour, moving in and out of his office. The principal then started to talk to Tony, and Tony maintained eye contact. Tony listened and was able to repeat concerns and issues about his inappropriate verbal behaviors. The principal even hesitated a few times, and Tony's response was, "I'm Listening!" The consistency of the principal had paid off. The next time Tony was brought to the office, the passive-aggressive mode vanished. The differential reinforcement technique used by the principal turned the tables and shifted a student-controlling situation into the hands of the administrator. Through differentially reinforcing other behaviors, Tony's poor eye contact shifted to attention and his verbal replies were more respectful.

Case of Lenny: Working in a Successful Learning Environment

Creating a successful environment for all students can be difficult. The wide range of abilities that are present, especially with students who exhibit serious behavior problems, poses a challenge to teachers (Ramsey, 1995). As a teacher for behaviorally and emotionally disturbed children, I have had academically gifted students reading three grades above grade level and learning-disabled students reading two to six grades below grade level. Differences in aptitude and reading level strikingly appeared in the case of Lenny.

Lenny, a student reading six grades below level, was a streetwise, popular young man 16 years old. To Lenny, his peers were very important, and losing face was something he could not let happen. Rather than read aloud, he would cause a behavior problem; his mischief would create a power struggle with the teacher and cause serious class disruption. Lenny's attention-seeking antics swiftly gained admiration from his peers and reinforced his persistency, intensity, and frequency of deviant remarks. Instinct compelled the teacher to remove Lenny from the class and thereby terminate peer reinforcement. But while removal from the classroom stopped disruption, it also removed Lenny from the primordial problem. His difficulty did not lay in wisecracking remarks. His difficulty was suffering embarrassment because he could not read.

Alternatively, I used a technique called *life-space interviewing*. This method involves having a dialogue, in private, about behaviors, goals, and procedures in the classroom. It is a *sharing experience*. I reveal personal or semipersonal information to elicit disclosures from the student. Both speaking truthfully and appearing vulnerable, Lenny and I *instantly bond in empathy without the formality and intimidation of authority-student roles*. The teacher asks questions, and the student is allowed to ask questions. The teacher may also share personal information that might give insight to the student's problems.

In this case, I shared my own reading problems when I was in high school. This seemed to open a door with Lenny that previously had been shut. The next day in class, the I also told the rest of my students about my reading difficulties when I was in high school. This established a link among Lenny, other students, and me. Most often, if a teacher had trouble reading and overcame it, it was very possible that the students could do the same. I had to create a safe environment where prestige or status with peers would not be lost. I pointed out that in my classroom, no one would be laughed at or snickered at when reading. Critics and teasers would receive consequences such as lunch detention or placed in a corner away from the other students. More than just a safe haven for reading, I assured Lenny he could expose his weakness with dignity.

I made sure that Lenny was given short passages to read and that he received help as soon as he stumbled on a word. When he read a few sentences without problems, he quickly received positive feedback and praise. The result was that Lenny, a tenth grader reading on a fourth grade level, jumped four grades in reading to an eighth grade level in just one year. By the time Lenny graduated, he was less than one grade level behind in reading. He was able to take the North Carolina Competency Test without modifications and received a full high school diploma.

Case of James: Enriching the Academically Gifted with Serious Behavior Problems

James was an academically gifted student who was three grade levels ahead in reading. Unlike Lenny, he presented a very different problem. Keeping him on-task was a challenge without being tempted to overassign him homework due to his accelerated aptitude. The solution lay in mainstreaming and movement throughout the day. Movement in regular as well as advanced placement classrooms was possible and first required his understanding of behavior expectancies in such classrooms. Elective reading class such as Literature in the 20th Century or

Science Fiction Literature required regular homework completion, silence during lecture, and nondisturbance of peers during the class.

A contract stating these behavior expectations in exchange for mainstreaming was put into effect. If negative or inappropriate behaviors occurred in mainstream classrooms, the contract would be considered violated and immediately result in loss of the mainstream class. Violated contracts also meant returning to the re-source room, which was unpleasant. To assure this, consequences such as loss of freedoms (e.g., closed lunch, not allowed to socialize at class changes) or restitutional acts (e.g., clean room, help other students) occurred within the first days of returning to resource classes. James was mainstreamed into one class at a time following a contract signed by him, his mother, and the facilitator of the con-tract. He eventually gained four out of six mainstreamed, advanced placement classes out the self-contained, core classroom.

Creating movement for students with serious behavior problems effectively de-celerates disruptive behavior but has several downsides. First, it takes extensive creativity and ingenuity. While educators may cleverly design a movement pro-gram, approval of this program through administration can take time. Adminis-trators will want these students kept in a core, resource classroom or designated areas of the school so that they will cause less trouble and not be in the public eye. A second problem is scheduling the students. Frequently, schedule changes can be done only at the quarter and not when the student's appropriate behavior warrants it. But worse than timing, assigned classrooms may inherently have structural de-fects. According to Wong et al. (1991), the classroom that may initially be given to students with behavior problems often may be inadequate in size and not suitable to their individual needs and lack stimulating cognitive challenges. Absence of these structural variables not only delays learning but also sets the stage for repeat opposition in class.

A third problem is student reputation. Unfortunately, the reputation of many special needs students precedes their arrival to class, and teachers inform you ahead of time they absolutely refuse admission of the students to their classes. Re-luctant teachers are vehemently pessimistic and may act on self-fulfilling prophe-cies to assure that the students fail miserably in their classes. Inadvertently, such teachers may sabotage these students' chances of success. Like teachers, many counselors in charge of scheduling may be reluctant to even discuss placing one of these students in a mainstream or advanced-level classroom. The administration, teachers, and counselors as well as the physical facility itself can pose major road-blocks in the process of movement for students with serious behavior and emo-tional problems.

Overcoming systemic-school obstacles is not an easy task but is a realistic one. Conroy and Fox (1994), for example, showed many ways to create and successfully implement schoolwide movement such as point systems, level systems, token economies, contracting, restricting freedoms, positive reinforcements, consequating, and mainstreaming, and integrating. Briefly reviewed is each meth-odology to see its potential value for inner-city, behaviorally disturbed students.

Point Systems

Point systems are an excellent means of documenting behaviors. An example of a point system would be to allot points for each period in the course (approximately 40 minutes) of a high school or middle school day. There should be five target behaviors stated on the point card: three general behaviors, such as following directions, staying on task and completing assignments; and two behaviors unique to the student's individual behavior problems. There can be a wide range of these targeted behaviors; however, they must be measurable and exhibited within the school setting (e.g., setting fires in the community would not be an appropriate individual targeted behavior).

The behaviors should be stated positively and should always be specific. Common targeted behaviors may be speaking appropriately or keeping hands and feet to oneself. There should be a set number of points (1 to 5) for each behavior listed. The total for one course could then be as much as 25 (see Figure 1).

Using Figure 1 as a guide, here is how the point system worked. If a student was in your homeroom and five core classes, then the maximum points for one day could be 300. A *passing or successful* day should earn 240 points, 80% of the maximum possible points for the day. For accountability purposes, it is not recommended that the actual point card be removed from the core setting. The possible inconsistencies of different teachers, loss of point sheet, destroying point sheets, or any other sabotage to the point sheet will bring on inconsistencies that will bring negative behaviors and lack of results within the point system.

A point system is an excellent tool to use to help shape behaviors and give immediate feedback to the students. I prefer to keep the point cards on my desk and record points myself. This leaves no margin for subjectivity or errors. Other teachers, teacher assistants, and behavior facilitators (e.g., behavior management technicians, counselors) may have the students keep the point cards on their desk, marking their own cards. While seemingly efficient, self-scoring cards run many risks of inaccuracy. I have tried this throughout the years, and the process was not smooth or successful. The students invariably lost cards, destroyed cards, added or erased marks, or caused other problems undermining accountability with the point system.

Level System

A level system restricts freedom, from the least possible restriction to the most restrictive containment. An example of this would be the *six-level* or *six-stair system*. On level 6, students have at least one mainstream/integrated class, freedom to change classes on their own, freedom to go to the rest room on their own, freedom to choose their own seat in class. On level 6, students can eat in the cafeteria with whom they choose as well as where they choose. These freedoms are not the legal rights of students in public school but are offered to students only if they can maintain appropriate behaviors within the school environment. On level 5, students have all the freedoms of level 6, but may not have a mainstream or integrated class.

Figure 1
Daily Behavior Card Used to Track Classroom Behavior Compliance During Entire School Day

Student: _____
Recording Teacher: _____

Date: _____
Total Points for Day: _____

Points 0–5

Behaviors	1	2	3	4	5	+	Comments
Following Directions							
Staying on Task							
Completing Assignments							
TOTALS							
Initials							

Forcing students into an advanced placement class or a mainstream class (out of a resource or self-contained program) may cause them to sabotage their new privileges and freedoms. As mentioned earlier, finding a class and teacher that students is comfortable with is the key to maintaining appropriate behavior and social skills. On level 4, all the freedoms of the preceding levels exist except that students have not earned a mainstreamed class. The key difference here is earning the privilege for a mainstream class, whereas in level 5, the mainstream class is not an earnable option. On level 3, students begin to lose freedom, mostly movement, outside the core classroom (including resource or self-contained program). Students on level 3 would be placed on escort to the rest room or anywhere else they had to go to during the course of the day. Closed lunch (no choice where or with whom students sit) is also part of level 3.

On level 2, students are on escort, are given an assigned seat apart from the rest of the class, and are also on closed lunch. There are no freedoms on this level such as mainstreamed/integrated classes, socialization, or most choices of any kind. On level 1, the most restrictive level, students are on escort and have an assigned seat and closed lunch, and the day is shortened. The shortened day would be a decision made with the administration, teacher, and parents or guardian. Usually, the shortened day is a brief period of time, due to the short motivation of teenagers to try to maintain appropriate behaviors to get back with their peer group. On level 1, transportation must be arranged and all student movement must be clear and precise to eliminate gray areas so students can move up to the next level within 10 to 15 school days.

Using a daily point sheet, daily appropriate and inappropriate behaviors are documented. The teacher, teacher assistant, or behavior facilitator within the school must be accountable for students' points so each child can trust the system and continue upward motion through the level system. Students would move up, move down, or maintain their level based on specific criteria such as grades, attendance, and appropriate behaviors on school campus. The criteria for the level system should be specific and explained to all children participating in this system. Most importantly, there should be no room for subjective decision making on the part of the teacher, counselor, administrator, or any authority, or the level system will not work. Also noteworthy is that a single untoward event should not cause a backward move in the level system. Any level system that involves mainstream classes can present potential problems. Pulling students in and out of classes should be done sparingly.

Any movement should be made clear to the student well in advance of its occurring. At the outset, begin students on level 4. Even then, even when student motivation and point structure are securely in place, implementation problems inevitably arise and should be handled efficiently.

Token Economies

Token economy systems are a useful tool in shaping behaviors toward long-term goals. This type of system is especially useful with younger children, kindergarten through seventh graders. Gaining points that can be converted to weekly, daily, or longer-term rewards may appeal to impulsive, self-gratifying thinking. A large variety of items can be used as positive reinforcers and are highly motivating; for example, inexpensive items such as stickers, erasers, pencils, pens, paper, notepads, sugar-free candy/gum, trading cards, makeup, hygiene products (samples), soda, balls, and so on. Almost all items used for token economy systems are obtainable from donations to the school from local businesses, outlets, manufacturing companies, and factories (e.g., cookie/bread factories, toy warehouses, soda factories, local team corporations). A few phone calls to the manager or supervisor, with a brief follow-up letter on school letterhead, usually bring the donations that are needed to start a token economy program in your class or school. Writing grants for small amounts will bring in enough money to buy a glass showcase or cabinet to lock up all merchandise yet display the items for purchase. Throughout the days, weeks, and months, students can view the merchandise that they can purchase, using their earned points. Visual stimuli can be powerful elicitors of behavior change and swiftly prompt appropriate behaviors. While clearly an asset, token economy systems can be misused or applied inconsistently. It is critical that points and positive reinforcers be given only only *when earned*. The giving of reinforcers when a negative behavior has occurred brings *only* more negative behaviors. Recording points, establishing their worth, and keeping all things accountable for exchanges in the school and class store are the key to a successful token economy system.

Contracting

Contracting with students, teachers, administrators, and other involved parties is an excellent method to use when trying to eliminate gray-area behaviors (e.g., tardy to class or talking back to authorities). It is also effective to utilize when specifying what *is* acceptable behavior. A contract acts as a catalyst when mainstreaming a student. The contract succinctly spells out appropriate behaviors, including homework, testing, and following class rules and procedures (e.g., raising hands to speak, sharpening pencils). This specific information assists the student to maintain and succeed in all regular classrooms (e.g., classes taught by regular teacher in classes of 20 or more students of all abilities).

Bardill (1977) states that an effective contract spells out information in language the student understands. Information clearly defined includes arriving on time to class, using a locker, receiving a passing grade, using "inside" voices (speaking in a lower voice more appropriate for communicating indoors), following teacher directions, as well as prohibiting any major inappropriate or negative behaviors (e.g., name-calling, fighting).

As in any effective program, strategy, or intervention for students with serious behavior and emotional disorders, contracts must be enforceable. The contract also protects the students from possible misunderstandings. Another positive use for contracting is to notify the student of possible consequences for negative behaviors if they recur. From a positive point of view, the contract states in advance the specific gains received for exhibiting positive behaviors. The most important rule in formulating contracts is that they must be concise, stated clearly, and viable within the school system.

Positive Reinforcement

Positive reinforcement, technically speaking, is the presentation, following a behavior, of any object or event that increases the future probability of that behavior. *Positive* means an object or event is literally concrete and given to the student. *Reinforcement* scientifically implies that the outcome of presenting this object or event to a student, not just once but frequently, is acceleration of some desired or target behavior. Often, more than one behavior is the beneficiary of reinforcement. Concurrent improvements occur over two or three behaviors, such as sitting quietly and on-task studying.

In an everyday sense, positive reinforcers are the foundation of learning. Stimulating skills through incentives creates more permanent effects than using no reinforcers or purely corrective feedback. This is because disputing students typically are byproducts of culturally deprived or aversive households and accustomed to punitive surroundings. Reliance on punishers produces habits and inappropriate behaviors that they already do at home and that contravene study skills. Reinforcers, on the other hand, represent a new and frequently enticing experience, holding the interest of even the most recalcitrant student.

Positive reinforcement can be accomplished in many different ways. Examples of positive reinforcement have been visible throughout the book, the most common of which include verbal praise and immediate gratifiers such as edibles or toys. Using a point system and level system with positive reinforcement, reinforcers can be given as earned free time, time on computer, or even mainstream classes. Working with individual teachers or staff members would also serve as positive reinforcement, such as assisting the art teacher, physical education teacher, or mechanics teacher. Elementary students with serious behavior problems are highly motivated to help school custodians or school secretaries. These are but a few of the possible gains or reinforcers that can be used to enhance positive behaviors.

The combination of rewards and consequences can be a powerful tool to change behaviors of students with serious behavior and emotional disorders. However, many pitfalls can occur when using these techniques due to a lack of consistency. The failure to follow through with consequences is the major trap that can befall many teachers and authority figures. Witt and Martens (1983) found that the most common mistakes made by teachers and administrators include ignoring inappropriate behaviors, threatening to give an unrealistic consequence (e.g., You're out of this school for good!") or threatening to give a consequence and not following through with it (e.g., "If you don't sit down, I'm calling the office; I will next time; don't make me call that office!"). Whenever the adult does not carry through with the consequence, the student is then in control, pushing and controlling the parameters of negative behaviors.

All children attempt to expand parameters of accepted behaviors, but children with serious behavior and emotional disorders engage in this practice with a high degree of persistence. Positive reinforcers and aversive consequences, more so than all other interventions, have the ability to change and shape behaviors on a short-term basis. The degree to which the teacher or administrator can consistently and immediately reinforce positive behavior or consequences, the greater the likelihood of effectively altering behaviors on a short-term basis. Therefore, all consequences used must follow a continuum of severity that gets stronger and more serious as the inappropriate behaviors are exhibited.

Mainstreaming

Mainstreaming is a term most recently used by teachers and administrators of exceptional children. The exceptional child is placed in a least restrictive classroom such as a class taught by a regular teacher. However, in a broader sense, mainstreaming can refer to any student, regardless of where he or she is on the continuum of programming within the school system.

Case in Point: Mainstreaming Tim and Greg

Tim and Greg, two sixth grade students with severe emotional and behavior disorders, were placed in a self-contained program on the same day. They were informed of the level system, the daily behavior program, and the rules and procedures for earning freedoms and mainstream classes. The level system used placed the students on level 4 when they entered the program. When directed by an authority figure, Tim, diagnosed as Attention Deficit Hyperactivity Disorder (ADHD) as well as Oppositional Defiant Disorder (ODD), tended to withdraw into a passive-aggressive state. Greg was also diagnosed as ADHD and ODD, but was very aggressive and acted out with his peers (e.g., verbally threatening, fighting).

After 15 days, Tim had minimal behavior problems and earned a mainstream class. He chose art and was highly motivated to keep his class and possibly add more and eventually approached and maintained the highest level, level 6. Greg, on the other hand, had a fight within the first three weeks and walked out of class. The combination of various behavior problems relegated Greg down a level, losing freedoms, to level 3. Greg was placed on escort everywhere he went. On the other hand, Tim was still maintaining appropriate behavior and good grades in his mainstream class and was ready to add another mainstream class. Tim was granted an academic mainstream, math, and was also given a contract specifying behaviors needed to maintain this class.

This intervention, mainstreaming and a contract, proved effective and successful. Soon, Tim was ready to exit the self-contained classroom and enter regular programming due to effectively responding to mainstream incentives and contracting to specify and regulate appropriate behaviors. Through periodic monitoring, short consulting session, and a consultative individual education plan (IEP) that stated short- and long-term goals, Tim achieved circulation in regular classrooms at the middle school. Greg, on the other hand, was not buying into the program, could not be motivated by earned freedoms, and was not intimidated by losing levels as well as freedoms within the school and classroom. Greg continued to pick fights and aggressively fight with peers. Even dropping him to level 1 failed to effect change.

The next move was a shortened day. Transportation was arranged, and Greg was escorted off school grounds after lunch. This was the final option before considering alternative programs or placements. It was evident that a more restrictive environment would be considered quickly, because a shortened day was not a long-standing option and not in the best interest of this student. A practical contract was developed that involved his teacher, administrators, Greg, and his parents. This contract was written with specific information about what was to happen if Greg could not alter his behavior with the support offered from his parents, teachers, and staff at the school. It was understood that this was the last intervention and that Greg would be placed out of the high school, away from his friends, into a more restrictive environment if there was no change in behavior. The contract stated positive changes such as lengthening his day slowly, as positive behaviors progressively occurred. One class period at a time would be added as Greg moved up the level system, demonstrating efforts in managing his aggressive behaviors. This strategy worked for Greg, *not because Greg wanted it to work but because the structure and reinforcers were tight, limited, and consistent.*

Although both Tim and Greg entered the program and the level system at the same time, they went in different directions due to various individual traits (i.e., self-motivation, home support, sense of failure, low self-esteem). The level system worked well with both students, regardless of their success or failure. Consistent movement of students in the level system can alter behavior in a variety of different ways, yet the end result or goal usually demonstrates a change in behavior.

Overall, level systems significantly manage misbehavior while promoting educational growth. They are economical, efficient, and likeable by most administrators and non-special education teachers. However, according to Gibbs and Luyben (1985), there are three major obstacles with the use of a level system. These include:

1. The consistency of the individual(s) in charge of making decision to move a student up or down a level.

2. A single event, either a positive or negative behavior, should not move a student up or down a level.

3. The lack of clear and precise guidelines for this movement can become a problem, as this type of student often expertly manipulates any kind of gray area without specific regulations for the move up or down a level.

Removal of potential pitfalls is an arduous process involving the uniformity of all personnel intimately connected with legislating the level program. When consistency is honored, and students follow relatively routine guidelines throughout the entire school, behavior change truly eventuates beyond expectations. One case in point is an effective token economy system modeled after the level system for a student named Darlene.

Darlene: Effective Token Economy Systems

Darlene, a passive-aggressive, withdrawn 11-year-old had been orphaned at the age of 5. She was a difficult child to reach. When she was exposed to a token economy, tied into the level system, she immediately bought into the intervention. The variety of positive reinforcers available, from personal hygiene products, to clothing or toys, all represented things that Darlene had very little of her own. The possibility of earning these items, through altered behaviors, worked her up the level system and had a positive emotional effect; it drew Darlene out of her shell. The point system, tying into the level system, allowed Darlene to continuously know where she stood each day. This, in turn, allowed her to become motivated to alter behaviors to reach an attainable goal.

The combination of interventions motivated trust in authority figures that could assist her to reach her goal. Her targeted behaviors included (1) maintaining eye contact when spoken to, (2) following directions, (3) participating in group situation, and (4) acknowledging authority figures. These behaviors were tied to the points earned. Utilizing this intervention, Darlene had a reasonable chance of unlimited reward-earning opportunities. However, availability of earnable tokens was not enough. *Motivation for involvement was necessary.* This was accomplished by actively involving her in the process. When Darlene first stepped into the school store, a metamorphosis took place. Darlene had her points in her hand and looked at the items with wide eyes. She asked if she could have certain items, wanting everything she saw. It was also the most communicative I had ever seen her. Darlene was hooked. How many points for the tiger shirt? I told her it would be 250 points. She had only 100. I suggested she save her points for a week or two until she had enough to buy that shirt.

She agreed. It didn't take long for Darlene to figure out that she could spend a little for the small items and take something home every week. In six months' time, she was following directions, talking with peers, and seeking out authority figures to assist her when she was in need.

In other words, Darlene received *reinforcement priming*, in which preliminary contact occurs with promised or earnable rewards under a controlled setting (the school store); access is limited only by the fact that students lack a response quota to immediately earn the reinforcers but now know what reinforcers they want. Reinforcement priming provides a second incentive of teaching realistic self-expectations. Students who set realistic goals to attain reinforcers can transfer this principle of self-motivation into other nontoken economy classrooms. Skill generalization without tokens is usually the bottom-line proof of an effective token economy or level system.

On a personal note, the ultimate reward of teaching high-risk students is seeing a student graduate who would have otherwise been a dropout, gone to prison, or wound up in the morgue. This type of success stays with a person all of his or her life. When educators can teach a student with whom very few teachers or administrators were successful, it is euphoric. *It is why I went into teaching.* It is not until one starts to attain success with students who have serious behavior disorders that credibility is gained, and teachers, administrators, and parents begin to believe that these students can really graduate if they try.

Administrators and educators dealing with seriously behaviorally disturbed students must understand the concepts and practical methods of consistency, movement, and success. These three areas are the main elements to any program or intervention that effectively alters behaviors. When implemented correctly, and visible signs of lasting progress are evident, students graduate to be productive citizens, and the school gets another trophy, so to speak, for a successful mission. Trophies for sports may never match the number of symbolic trophies achieved for graduating troubled students. But the school, teachers, and parents know the trophy exists and feel the one thing so often missing in today's urban schools is: *belief in doing well.* Schools win unspoken accolades when they use *the right procedure, in the right way, and for the right reasons.*

NOTE

Editors' note: This author presents a personal account of directly managing severely disruptive classroom behaviors in high-risk, inner-city students diagnosed with behavioral disorders. Due to the significantly effective impact of his interventions, we requested this author to prepare his chapter through a personal as well as scholarly perspective.

REFERENCES

Akhtar, N., & Bradley, E. (1991). Social information processing deficits of aggressive children: Present findings and implications for social skills training. *Clinical Psychology Review*, 11, 621–644.

Alberto, P., & Troutman, A. (1995). *Applied behavior analysis for teachers* (4th ed.). Englewood Cliffs, NJ: Prentice-Hall.

Allen, L. J., Howard, V. F., Sweeney, W. J., & McLaughlin, T. F. (1983). Use of contingency contracting to increase on-task behavior with primary students. *Psychological Reports*, 73, 905–906.

Arter, J. A., & Spandel, V. (1992). Using portfolios of students' work in instruction and assessment. *Educational Measurement Issues and Practice*, 10, 36–51.

Athanases, S. Z., Christiano, D., & Lay, E. (1995). Fostering empathy and finding common ground in multiethnic classes. *English Journal*, 26–34.

Ball, E., & Harry, B. (1993). Multicultural education and special education: Parallels, divergences, and intersections. *Education Forum*, 57, 430–436.

Bangert-Drowns, R. L. (1993). The word processor as an instructional tool: A meta-analysis of word processing in writing instruction. *Review of Education Research*, 63, 69–93.

Banks, J. A. (1994a). *An introduction to multicultural education*. Boston: Allyn & Bacon.

Banks, J. A. (1994b). *Multiethnic education: Theory and practice* (3rd ed.). Boston: Allyn & Bacon.

Bardill, D. R. (1977). A behavior contracting program of group treatment for early adolescents in a residential treatment setting. *International Journal of Group Psychotherapy*, 27, 389–400.

Bauer, N. J. (1993). *Instructional designs, portfolios and the pursuit of authentic assessment.* Paper presented at the spring conference of the New York State Association of Teacher Educators, Syracuse, NY.

Beck, R., & Gabriel, S. (1990). *Project RIDE: Responding to Individual Differences in Education (Elementary and Secondary Version)*. Longmont, CO: Sopris West.

Bennett, D., & Hawkins, J. (1993). Alternative assessment and technology. *News from the Center for Children and Technology and the Center for Technology in Education,* 1 (3), 4–194.

Bennett, E., Rock, D. A., & Wang, M. W. (1991). Equivalence of free-response and multiple-choice items. *Journal of Educational Measurement,* 28 (1), 77–92.

Bergan, J., & Caldwell, T. (1995). Operant techniques in school psychology. *Journal of Educational and Psychological Consultation,* 6, 103–110.

Bickel, W. E., & Bickel, D. D. (1986). Effective schools, classrooms, and instruction: Implications for special education. *Exceptional Children,* 52, 489–500.

Bijou, S. W. (1975). Moral development in the preschool years: A functional analysis. *Mexican Journal of Behavior Analysis,* 1, 11–29.

Billingsley, B. S., & Cross, L. H. (1991). Teachers' decision to transfer from special to general education. *Journal of Special Education,* 24, 496–511.

Boe, E. E., & Church, R. M. (1968). *Punishment.* New York: Appleton-Century-Crofts.

Boonin, T. (1979). The benighted status of U.S. school corporal punishment practice. *The Kappan,* 5, 395–396.

Bourg, S., & Stock, H. V. (1994). A review of domestic violence arrest statistics in a police department using a pro-arrest policy: Are pro-arrest policies enough? *Journal of Family Violence,* 9, 177–189.

Braaten, S. (1987). *Use of punishment with exceptional children: A dilemma for educators.* Paper presented at the 11th Conference on Severe Behavior Disorders of Children and Youth, Tempe, AZ.

Broome, S. A., & White, R. B. (1995). The many uses of videotape in classrooms serving youth with behavioral disorders. *Teaching Exceptional Children,* 27, 10–13.

Brophy, J. (1988). Teacher praise: A functional analysis. *Review of Educational Research,* 51, 5–32.

Broussard, C., & Northrup, J. (1997). The use of functional analysis to develop peer interventions for disruptive classroom behavior. *School Psychology Quarterly,* 12, 65–76.

Bruder, I. (1993). Alternative assessment: Putting technology to the test. *Electronic Learning,* 12(4), 22–23.

Burchard, J. D., & Harig, P. T. (1976). Behavior modification and juvenile delinquency. In H. Leitenberg (Ed.), *Handbook of behavior modification and behavior therapy* (pp. 405–452). Englewood Cliffs, NJ: Prentice-Hall.

Burchard, J. D., & Lane, T. W. (1982). Crime and delinquency. In A. S. Bellack, M. Hersen, and A. E. Kazdin (Eds.), *International handbook of behavior modification and therapy* (pp. 613–652). New York: Plenum Press.

Campbell, R., Cunningham, L., Nystrand, R., Usdan, M. (1990). *The Organization and control of American schools.* Columbus, OH: Merrill Publishing Co.

Canter, L., & Canter, M. (1993). *Succeeding with difficult students.* Los Angeles, CA: Canter & Associates.

Carpenter, S. L., & McKee-Higgins, E. (1996). Behavior management in inclusive classrooms. *Remedial and Special Education,* 17, 195–203.

Carr, E. G., Levin, L., McConnachie, G., Carlson, J. L., Kemp, D. C., & Smith, C. E. (1994). *Communication-based intervention for problem behavior: A user's guide for producing change.* Baltimore, MD: Baltimore Public Schools.

Chapman, J. W. (1988). Cognitive-motivational characteristics and academic achievement of learning disabled children: A longitudinal study. *Journal of Educational Psychology,* 80 (3), 357–365.

Choate, J. S., & Miller, L. J. (1992). Curricular assessment and programming. In J. S. Choate, Enright, L. J. Miller, J. A. Poteet, & T. Rakes (1992). *Curriculum-based assessment and programming*. Needham, MA: Allyn & Bacon.

Clarke, S., Dunlap, G., Foster-Johnson, L., Childs, K., Wilson, D., & Vera, A. (1995). Improving the conduct of students with behavioral disorders by incorporating student interests into curricular activities. *Behavioral Disorders*, 20 (4), 221–237.

Cochran-Smith, M. (1991). Word processing and writing in elementary classrooms: A critical review of related literature. *Review of Educational Research*, 61, 107–155.

Cohen, M. W. (1986). Intrinsic motivation in the special education classroom. *Journal of Learning Disabilities*, 19 (5), 258–261.

Collis, B., & Heeren, E. (1993). Tele-collaboration and groupware. *The Computing Teacher*, 5, 36–39.

Colvin, G., Kameenui, R. J., & Sugai, G. (1993). Reconceptualizing behavior management and school-wide discipline in general education. *Education and Treatment of Children*, 16, 361–381.

Conley, R. W., & Noble, J. H. (1990). Benefit cost analysis of supported employment. In F. R. Rusch (Ed.), *Supported employment: Models, methods, and issues* (pp. 271–288). Sycamore, IL: Sycamore.

Conroy, M. A., & Fox, J. J. (1994). Setting events and challenging behaviors in the classroom: Incorporating contextual factors into effective intervention plans for children with aggressive behaviors. *Preventing School Failure*, 38, 29–34.

Curwin, R., & Mendler, A. (1988). *Discipline with dignity*. Alexandria, VA: Association for Supervision and Curriculum Development. (ERIC Document Service Reproduction No. ED 302-938)

Dale, E. J. (1993). *Computers and exceptional individuals*. Austin, TX.: PRO-ED.

D'Alonzo, B. J., Fass, L. A., & Crawford, D. (1988). School to work transition: Project M.E.A.L. model for employment and adult living. *Career Development for Exceptional Individuals*, 11, 126–140.

Davey, B., & Rindone, D. A. (1990). *Anatomy of a performance task*. Paper presented at the American Education Research Association Annual Meeting, Boston.

Delprato, D. J. (1980). The reactional biography concept: Early contributions to a perspective for the psychology of aging. *Human Development*, 23, 314–322.

Delprato, D. J. (1986). Response patterns. In. H. W. Reese & L. J. Parrott (Eds.), *Behavior science: Philosophical, methodological and empirical advances* (pp. 61–113). Hillsdale, NJ: Lawrence Erlbaum Associates.

Delprato, D. J. (1987). Developmental interactionism: An integrative framework for behavior therapy. *Advances in Behaviour Research and Therapy*, 9, 173–205.

Delprato, D. J., & McGlynn, F. D. (1986). Innovations in behavioral medicine. In M. Hersen, R. M. Eisler & P. M. Miller (Eds.), *Progress in behavior modification*, vol. 30 (pp. 67–122). Orlando, FL: Academic Press.

Deutsch, M. (1979). Education and distributive justice. *American Psychologist*, 34 (5), 391–401.

Dougherty, D. M., Cherek, D. R., & Lane, S. D. (1998). Aggressive responding in the laboratory maintained by the initiation of a provocation-free interval. *Psychological Record*, 48, 591–600.

Dreikurs, R., Grunwalk, B., & Pepper, F. (1982). *Maintaining sanity in the classroom*. New York: Harper & Row.

Durante, J. E. (1993). Attributions for achievement outcomes among behavioral subgroups of children with learning disabilities. *Journal of Special Education*, 27, 306–320.

Elam, S., Rose, L., & Gallup, A. (1996). The 28th annual Phi Delta Kappan Gallup poll of the public's attitudes toward the public schools. *Phi Delta Kappan*, 26, 32–36.

Elliott, B. A. (1993). Community responses to violence. *Primary Care*, 20, 495–502.

Emmer, E. T., Evertson, C. M., Sanford, J. P., Clements, B. S., & Worsham, M. E. (1989). *Classroom management for secondary teachers* (2nd ed.). Englewood Cliffs, NJ: Prentice-Hall.

ERIC Clearinghouse on Reading and Communication Skills, Bloomington, IN.

Espinola, O. (1992). *A user's guide to Braille'n Speak*. Forest Hill, MD: Blazie Engineering.

Fagen, S. A., Long, N. J., & Stevens, D. J. (1975). *Teaching children self-control: Preventing emotional and learning problems in the elementary school*. Columbus, OH: Merrill.

Farr, R. (1991). Portfolios: Assessment in language arts. (Report No. EDO-CS-91-09).

Ferrara, R. A. (1987). Learning mathematics in the zon of proximal development: The importance of flexible use of knowledge. Unpublished doctoral dissertation, University of Illinois, Urbana-Champaign.

Fimian, M. J. (1983). A comparison of occupational stress correlates as reoprted by teachers of mentally retarded and nonmentally retarded handicapped students. *Education and Training of the Mentally Retarded*, 18, 62–68.

Finn, Jeremy D. (1989). Withdrawing from school. *Review of Educational Research*, 59, 117–142.

Fox, J., & Conroy, M. (1995). Setting events and behavioral disorders of children and youth: An interbehavioral field analysis for research and practice. *Journal of Emotional and Behavioral Disorders*, 3, 130–140.

Fuchs, L. S., & Deno, S. L. (1991). Paradigmatic distinctions between instructionally relevant measurement models. *Exceptional Children*, 57, 488–500.

Gable, R. A., Enright, B. E., & Hendrickson, J. (1991). A practical model for curriculum-based assessment and instruction in arithmetic. *Teaching Exceptional Children*, 24 (1), 6–9.

Gibbs, J. W., & Luyben, P. D. (1985). Treatment of self-injurious behavior: contingent versus noncontingent positive practice overcorrection. *Behavior Modification*, 9 (1), 3–21.

Glasser, W. (1988). *Schools without failure*. New York: Harper & Row.

Glenn, C. L. (1989). Just schools for minority children. *Phi Delta Kappan*, 10, 777–779.

Glenn, H. S., & Nelson, J. (1987). *Raising self-reliant children in a self-indulgent world*. Rocklin, CA: Prima.

Gold, M., & Mann, D. W. (1982). Alternative schools for troublesome secondary students. *The Urban Review*, 14, 305–316.

Goldstein, A. (1994). *Student aggression: Prevention, management, and replacement training*. New York: Longman.

Gollnick, D. M., & Chinn, P. C. (1994). *Multi-cultural education in a pluralistic society* (4th ed.). Englewood Cliffs, NJ: Merrill/Prentice-Hall.

Good, T., & Brophy, J. (1990). *Educational psychology: A realistic approach* (4th ed.). Reading, MA: Addison Wesley. (ERIC Document Reproduction Service No. ED 314367).

Gorton, R. (1983). *School administration and supervision*. Dubuque, IA: Brown.

Grady, E. (1992). *The portfolio approach to assessment*. (Report No. 0-87367-341-7). Phi Delta Kappa Educational Foundation. Bloomington, IN. ERIC Document (Reproduction Service No. ED 356273).

Greer, J. G., & Greer, B. B. (1992). Stopping burnout before it starts: Prevention measures at the preservice level. *Teacher Education and Special Education*, 15, 168–174.

Gresham, F. M., & Reshcly, D. J. (1987). Issues in the conceptualization, classification, and assessment of social skills in the mildly handicapped. In T. R. Kratochwill (Ed.), *Advances in school psychology*, vol. 6 (pp. 203–247). Hillsdale, NJ: Lawrence Erlbaum Associates.

Griffin, D. K. (1998). A survey of common behavioral procedures used by exceptional educational teachers in the greater Miami/Ft. Lauderdale, Fl. area public schools. *The Behavior Therapist*, 21, 163–165, 193.

Grossman, H. (1990). *Classroom behavior management in a diverse society*. Mountain View, CA: Mayfield.

Grossman, H. J. (1995). *Teaching in a diverse society*. Boston, MA: Allyn & Bacon.

Gunter, P. L., Denny, R. K., Shores, R. E., Reed, T. M., Jack, S. L., & Nelson, M. (1994). Teacher escape, avoidance and countercontrol behaviors: Potential responses to disruptive and aggressive behaviors of students with severe behavior disorders. *Journal of Child and Family Studies*, 3, 211–223.

Hall, H. V., & Whitaker, L. C. (Eds.). (1998). *Effective strategies for assessing and intervening in fatal group and institutional aggression*. Boca Raton, FL: CRC Press.

Halpern, A. S. (1990). Transition: Old wine in new bottles. *Exceptional Children*, 58, 202–211.

Hargrove, L. J., & Poteet, J. A. (1984). *Assessment in special education: The educational evaluation*. Englewood Cliffs, NJ: Prentice-Hall.

Hayes, L. A. (1976). The use of group contingencies for behavioral control: A review. *Psychological Bulletin*, 83, 628–648.

Hearne, J. (1992). Portfolio assessment: Tracking its implementation and use in one elementary school. In J. Bamberg (Ed.), *Assessment: How do we know what they know?* Union, WA: Association for Supervision and Curriculum Development.

Hersen, M. (1976). Limitations and problems in the clinical application of behavioral techniques in psychiatric settings. *Behavior Therapy*, 10, 65–80.

Higgins, K., & Boone, R. (1993). Technology as a tutor, tool, and agent for reading. *Journal of Special Education Technology*, 12, 28–37.

Hinkle, D., Wiersma, W., & Jurs, S. (1988). *Applied statistics for the behavioral sciences*. Boston: Houghton Mifflin.

Hodges, H., & Webb, L. (1996). Model schools in urban settings. *Quality education for minorities network*. Washington, DC: University Press of America.

Hopkins, K., & Glass, G. (1978). *Basic statistics for the behavioral sciences*. Englewood Cliffs, NJ: Prentice-Hall.

Horner, R. H., O'Neill, R. E., & Flannery, K. B. (1994). Effective behavior support plans. In M. E. Snell (Ed.), *Instruction of students with severe disabilities* (pp. 184–214). New York: Macmillan.

Huesmann, L. R., Maxwell, C. D., Eron, L., Dahlberg, L. L., Guerra, N. G., Tolan, P. H., VanAcker, R., & Henry, D. (1996). Evaluating a cognitive/ecological program for the prevention of aggression among urban children. *American Journal of Preventive Medicine*, 12, 120–128.

Hunter, M. (1982). *Mastery teaching*. El Segundo, CA: TIP.

Jaschik, S. (1990). U.S. court rules that requiring multiple-choice tests may violate the rights of learning-disabled students. *Chronicle of Higher Education*, 40, A17–A20.

Johns, B. H., & Carr, V. G. (1995). *Techniques for managing verbally and physically aggressive students*. Denver: Love.

Johnson, L. J., & Pugach, M. C. (1996). Role of collaborative diagnosis in teachers' conceptions of appropriate practice for students at risk. *Journal of Educational and Psychological Consultation, 7,* 9–24.

Johnston, J. M., & Pennypacker, H. S. (1980). *Strategies and tactics of human behavioral research.* Hillsdale, NJ: Lawrence Erlbaum Associates.

Jones, B. H., & Carr, V. G. (1995). *Techniques for managing verbally and physically aggressive students.* Denver, CO: Love.

Jones, V., & Jones, L. (1981). *Responsible classroom discipline.* New York: Allyn & Bacon.

Kameenui, E. J., & Darch, C. B. (1994). *Instructional classroom management.* White Plains, NY: Longman.

Kameenui, E. J., & Darch, C. B. (1995). *Instructional classroom management: A proactive approach to behavior management.* Reston, VA Council for Exceptional Children.

Kantor, J. R. (1970). An analysis of the experimental analysis of behavior (TEAB). *Journal of the Experimental Analysis of Behavior, 13,* 101–108.

Kazdin, A. E. (1975). *Behavior modification in applied settings.* Homewood, IL: Dorsey.

Kazdin. A. E. (1985). Selection of target behaviors: The relationship of the treatment focus to clinical dysfunction. *Behavioral Assessment, 7,* 33–47.

Kelly, B., Carnine, D., Gersten, R., & Grossen, B. (1987). The effectiveness of videodisc instruction in teaching fractions to learning handicapped and remedial high school students. *Journal of Special Education Technology, 8* (2), 5–17.

Kerr, M. M., & Nelson, C. M. (1998). *Strategies for managing behavior problems in the classroom.* Columbus, OH: Merrill.

Kunkel, J. H. (1983). The behavioral-societal approach to social problems. *Behaviorists for Social Action Journal, 4,* 8–11.

LaVigna, G. W., & Donnellan, A. M. (1986). *Alternatives to punishment: Solving behavior problems through non-aversive strategies.* New York: Irvington.

Lawrenson, G. M., & McKinnon, A. J. (1982). A survey of classroom teachers of the emotionally disturbed: Attrition and burnout factors. *Behavior Disorders, 8,* 41–49.

Lewis, A. C. (1990). Getting unstuck: Curriculum as a tool of reform. *Phi Delta Kappan, 71,* 534–538.

Lewis, R. B. (1993). *Special education technology: Classroom applications.* Pacific Grove, CA: Brookes.

Lewis, T. (1997). *Responsible decision making about effective behavioral support.* Available through the ERIC clearinghouse.

Licht, B. G., & Dweck, C. S. (1984). Determinants of academic achievement: The interaction of children's achievement orientations with skill areas. *Developmental Psychology, 20,* 628–636.

Locke, D. C. (1997). *Increasing multicultural understanding.* Thousand Oaks, CA: Sage.

Long, N. J., & Morse, W. C. (1996). *Conflict in the classroom.* Austin, TX: PRO-ED.

Macciomei, N. R. (1992). Freestyle writing: A three-phase expressive writing activity, *Teaching Exceptional Children, 24* (3), 53–54.

Maddux, C. D., Johnson, D. L., & Willis, J. W. (1992). *Educational computing: Learning with tomorrow's technologies.* Boston, MA: Allyn & Bacon.

Majsterek, D. J. (1990). Writing disabilities: Is word processing the answer? *Intervention in School and Clinic, 26,* 93–97.

Markus, H. R., & Kitayama, S. (1998). The cultural psychology of personality. *Journal of Cross-Cultural Psychology, 1,* 63–87.

Marlatt, G. A., & Gordon, J. R. (Eds.). *Relapse prevention.* New York: Guilford Press.

Martella, R. C., Marchand-Martella, N. E., Young, R. K., & Macfarlane, C. A. (1995). Determining the collateral effects of peer tutor training on student with severe disabilities. *Behavior Modification*, 19, 170–191.

McLoughlin, J., & Lewis, R. (1990). *Assessing special students*. New York: Macmillan.

McClure, R. M. (1992). *Alternative forms of student assessment*. Paper presented at the Annual Meeting of the American Educational Research Association, San Francisco (ERIC Document Reproduction Service No. ED 347 209).

McGrew-Zoubi, R., and Brown, G. (1995). Successful teaching in culturally diverse classrooms. *The Delta Kappa Gamma Bulletin*, 61, (2), 7–12.

Mercer, C. D., & Mercer, A. R. (1993). Teaching students with learning problems (4th ed.). New York: Merrill/Macmillan.

Meyer, C. A. (1992). What's the difference between authentic and performance assessment? *Educational Leadership*, 49 (8), 39–40.

Michael, J. (1982). Distinguishing between discriminative and motivational functions of stimuli. *Journal of the Experimental Analysis of Behavior*, 37, 149–155.

Michael, J. (1983). Evocative and repertoire altering effects of an environmental event. *VB News*, 2, 21–23.

Mickler, M. L., & Chaper, A. C. (1989). Basic skills in college: Academic solution or dilution? *Journal of Developmental Education*, 13, 2–6.

Moore, S. C., Agran, M., & McSweyn, C. A. (1990). Career education: Are we starting early enough? *Career Development for Exceptional Individuals*, 13, 129–134.

Morgan, T. D. (1993). Technology: An essential tool for gifted & talented education. *Journal for the Education of the Gifted*, 16 (4), 358–371.

Myles, B., & Simpson, R. (1994). Understanding and preventing acts of aggression and violence in school-age children and youth. *Preventing School Failure*, 38 (3), 40–46.

National Crisis Prevention Institute. (1983). *Nonviolent crisis intervention*. Washington, DC: Council of Education.

Nelson, J. (1987). *Positive discipline*. New York: Random House.

Nelson, J. R., Colvin, G., Petty, D., & Smith, D. J. (1995). The effects of a school-wide instructional discipline program on students' social behavior in common areas of the school. Unpublished manuscript, Washington University.

Nietzel, N. T. (1979). *Crime and its modification: A social learning perspective*. New York: Plenum.

Novelli, J. (1994). How to finally get comfortable with your computer. Instructor, 6, 68–72.

Office of Juvenile Justice and Delinquency Prevention. (1995). *Guide for implementing a comprehensive strategy for serious, violent and chronic juvenile offenders*. Washington DC: U.S. Department of Justice.

O'Leary, K. D., Kaufman, K. F., Kass, R. E., & Drabman, R. S. (1970). The effects of loud and soft reprimands on the behavior of disruptive students. *Exceptional Children*, 37, 145–155.

O'Leary, K. D., & O'Leary, S. G. (Eds.). (1976). *Classroom management: The successful use of behavior modification*. New York: Pergamon Press.

Olson, L., & P. Jerald, (1998). The challenges. Quality counts: Barriers to success. *Education Week*, 3, 12–45.

Patterson, G., & Reid, J. (1970). Reciprocity and coercion: Two facets of social systems. In C. Neuringer & J. L. Michael (Eds.), *Behavior modification in clinical psychology* (pp. 133–177). New York: Appleton.

Patterson, G., Reid, J., & Dishion, T. (1992). *Antisocial boys*. Eugene, OR: Castalia.

Phi Delta Kappa Commission on Discipline. (1982). *Handbook for developing schools with good discipline.* Bloomington, IN: Phi Delta Kappa.

Polsgrove, L., & Nelson, C. M. (1982). Curriculum interventions according to the behavioral model. In R. L. Mcdowell, F. H. Wood, & G. Adamson, (Eds.), *Teaching emotionally disturbed children* (169–206). Boston: Little, Brown.

Pophan, W. J. (1985). Measurement-driven instruction: It's on the road. *Phi Delta Kappan,* 66, 628–629.

Porterfield, J. K., Herbert-Jackson, E., & Risley, T. R. (1976). Contingent observation: An effective and acceptable procedure for reducing disruptive behavior of young children in a group setting. *Journal of Applied Behavior Analysis,* 9, 55–63.

Poteet, J. A., Choate, J. S., & Stewart, S. C. (1993). Performance assessment and special education practices and prospects, *Focus on Exceptional Children,* 26 (1), 1–20.

Ramsey, E. (1995). *Antisocial behavior in school: Strategies and best practices.* Pacific Grove, CA: Brooks/Cole.

Resnick, L. B., & Resnick, D. P. (1985). Standards, curriculum and performance: A historical and comparative perspective. *Educational Researcher,* 14, 5–21.

Reynolds, C. R. (1992). Two key concepts in the diagnosis of learning disabilities and the habilitation of learning. *Learning Disability Quarterly,* 15, 2–12.

Rhode, G., Jenson, W. R., & Reavis, H. K. (1993). *The tough kid book: Practical classroom management strategies.* Longmont, CO: Sopris West.

Ringler, L. (1992). Foreword. In A. A. DeFire, *Portfolio assessment: Getting started.* New York: Scholastic.

Rivard, J. D. (1997). *Quick guide to the Internet for educators.* Boston, MA: Allyn & Bacon.

Rogers, H., & Saklofske, D. H. (1985). Self-concepts, locus of control and performance expectations of learning disabled children. *Journal of Learning Disabilities,* 18, 273–278.

Rojewski, J. (1992). Key components of model transition services for students with learning disabilities. *Learning Disability Quarterly,* 15, 135–150.

Rosenshine, B., & Stevens, R. (1986). Teaching functions. In M. C. Wittrock (Ed.). *Handbook of research on teaching* (3rd ed.) (pp. 376–431). New York: Macmillan.

Rosenthal, I. (1989). Model transition programs for learning disabled high school and college students. *Rehabilitation Counseling Bulletin,* 33, 54–66.

Rothman, W. R., & Cohen, J. (1988). Teaching test taking skills. *Academic Therapy,* 23, 341–349.

Ruben, D. H. (1983). Interbehavioral implications for behavior therapy: Clinical perspectives. In N. Smith, P. T. Mountjoy, & D. H. Ruben (Eds.), *Reassessment in psychology: The Interbehavioral alternative* (pp. 445–469). Washington, DC: University Press of America.

Ruben, D. H. (1986). The "Interbehavioral" approach to treatment. *Journal of Contemporary Psychotherapy,* 16, 62–71.

Ruben, D. H. (1987). On the origins of selfishness. *Behavioural approaches with children,* 11, 116–127.

Ruben, D. H. (1990). *The aging and drug effects: A planning manual for medication and alcohol abuse treatment of the elderly.* Jefferson, NC: McFarland.

Ruben, D. H. (1992). Interbehavioral analysis of adult children of alcoholics: Etiological predictors. *Alcoholism Treatment Quarterly,* 9, 1–21.

Ruben, D. H. (1993a). *Avoidance syndrome: Doing things out of fear.* St. Louis, MO: Warren Green.

Ruben, D. H. (1993b). Transition failures in alcohol and drug abuse treatment. In D. H. Ruben & C. E. Stout (Eds.), *Transitions: Handbook of managed care for inpatient and outpatient treatment* (pp. 115–134). New York: Praeger.

Ruben, D. H. (1998). Social exchange theory: Dynamics of a system governing the dysfunctional family and guide to assessment. *Journal of Contemporary Psychotherapy, 28,* 307–325.

Ruben, D. H., & Ruben, M. J. (1985). Interviewing skills: Implications for vocation counseling with alcoholic clients. *Alcoholism Treatment Quarterly,*1, 133–140.

Ruben, D. H., & Ruben, M. J. (1987). Assumptions about teaching assertiveness: Training the person or behavior? In D. H. Ruben & D. J. Delprato (Eds.), *New ideas in therapy: Introduction to an interdisciplinary approach* (pp. 107–118). Westport, CT: Greenwood Press.

Rutherford, R. B., & Nelson, C. M. (1995). Management of aggressive and violent behavior in the schools. *Focus on Exceptional Children, 27,* 1–15.

Sajwaj, T. (1977). Issues and implications of establishing guidelines for the use of behavioral techniques. *Journal of Applied Behavior Analysis, 10,* 531–540.

Salvia, J., & Ysseldyke, J. E. (1984*). Assessment in special and remedial education.* Boston, MA: Houghton-Mifflin.

Schloss, P. J., Smith, M. A., & Scholss, C. N. (1990) *Instructional methods for adolescents with learning and behavior problems.* Boston: Allyn & Bacon.

Selby, D., & Murphy, S. (1992). Graded or degraded: Perceptions of letter-grading for mainstreamed learning-disabled students. *BC Journal of Special Education, 16* (1), 92–104.

Sheingold, K. (1991). Restructuring for learning with technology: The potential for synergy. *Phi Delta Kappan, 73,* 17–27.

Shepard, L. A. (1991). Psychometrician's beliefs about learning. *Educational Researcher, 20*(7), 2–16.

Shephard, L. A., & Smith, M. (1988). *Flunking grades: Research and policies on retention.* Philadelphia, PA: Falmer Press.

Sheppo, K. G., Hartsfield, S. J., Ruff, S., Jones, C. A., & Holinga, M. (1995). How an urban school promotes inclusion. *Educational Leadership, 53* (4), 82–83.

Shores, R. E. (1993). *General classroom management strategies: Are they effective with violent and aggressive students?* Paper presented at the Council for Exceptional children Annual convention, San Antonio, TX.

Shores, R. E., Gunter, P. L., Denny, R. K., & Jack, S. L. (1993). Classroom influences on aggressive and disruptive behaviors of students with emotional and behavioral disorders. *Focus on Exceptional Children, 26*(2), 1–10.

Shores, R. E., Jack, S. L. Gunter, P. L., Ellis, D. N., DeBriere, T., & Welby, J. (1993). Classroom interactions of children with severe behavior disorders. *Journal of Emotional and Behavioral Disorders, 1,* 27–39.

Siegel, S., Greener, K., & Robert, M. (1990). The career ladder program. *Interchange, 10,* 1–3.

Skinner, B. F. (1972). *Cumulative record* (p. 227). New York: Appleton-Century-Crofts.

Slavin, R. E. (1990). *Cooperative learning: Theory, research, and practice.* Englewood Cliffs, NJ: Prentice-Hall.

Smith, C. B. (1991). (Ed.). *Alternative assessment of performance in the language arts.* Bloomington, IN: ERIC Clearinghouse on Reading and Communication Skills.

Smith, S. W., & Farrell, D. T. (1993). Level system use in special education: Classroom intervention with prima facie appeal. *Behavioral Disorders, 18,* 92–102.

Smith, T. E. C., Polloway, E. A., Patton, J. R., & Dowdy, C. A. (1998). *Teaching students with special needs in inclusive settings.* Needham Heights, MA: Allyn & Bacon.

Staub, R. W. (1987). *The effects of publicly posted feedback on middle school students' disruptive hallway behavior.* Unpublished doctoral dissertation, University of Pittsburgh.

Steere, D., Pancsofar, E., Wood, R., & Hecimovic, A. (1990). Principles of shared responsibility. *Career Development for Exceptional Individuals, 13,* 143–153.

Stephens, R. (1995). *Safe schools: A handbook for violence prevention.* Bloomington, IN: National Educational Services.

Stiggins, R. J. (1987). Design and development of performance assessments. *Educational Measurement: Issues and Practice, 6* (3), 33–42.

Stokes, T. F., & Baer, D. M. (1977). An implicit technology of generalization. *Journal of Applied Behavior Analysis, 10,* 349–367.

Sugai, G. (1995). *Pro-active classroom management.* Workshop presented at the Springfield School Improvement Conference, Springfield, OR.

Sugai, G. M., & Tindal, G. A. (1993). *Effective school consultation: An interactive approach.* Pacific Grove, CA: Brooks/Cole.

Sulzer-Azaroff, B., & Mayer, G. R. (1972). *Behavior modification procedures for school personnel.* Hinsdale, IL: Dryden Press.

Swick, J. (1987). *Student stress: A classroom management system.* Washington, DC: National Education Association (ERIC Document Reproduction Service No. ED 307 514).

Taylor-Greene, S., Brown, D., Nelson, L., & Longton, J. (1997). School-wide behavioral support: Starting the year off right. *Journal of Behavioral Education, 7,* 99–112.

Terwillinger, J. S. (1971). *Assigning grades to students.* Glenview, IL: Scott, Foresman.

Test, D. W., Keul, P. K., & Grossi, T. (1988). Transitional services for mildly handicapped youth. *The Journal of Vocational Special Needs Education, 11,* 7–11.

Thomas, C. C., Correa, V. I., & Morsink, C. V. (1995). *Interactive teaming: Consultation and collaboration in special programs* (2nd ed.). Englewood Cliffs, NJ: Merrill/Prentice-Hall.

Tierney, R. J. (1992). Portfolios: Windows on learning-setting a new agenda for assessment *Learning, 54,* 61–64.

Tierney, R. J., Carter, M. A., & Desai, L. E. (1991). *Portfolio assessment in the reading-writing classroom.* Norwood, MA: Christopher Gordon.

Trotter, A. (1991). The sky's the limit when super students meet supercomputers. *Executive Educator, 13* (2), 17–18.

Turnbull, A. P., Turnbull, H. R., Shank, M., & Leal, D. (1995). *Exceptional lives: Special education in today's schools.* Englewood Cliffs, NJ: Prentice-Hall.

Valencia, S. (1990). A portfolio approach to classroom reading assessment: The whys, whats, and hows. *The Reading Teacher, 43,* 338–340.

Van Hasselt, V. B., & Hersen, M. (Eds.). (1998). *Handbook of psychological approaches with violent offenders.* New York: Plenum.

Van Houten, R., Nau, P. A., MacKenzie-Keating, S. E., Sameoto, D., & Colavecchia, B. (1982). An analysis of some variables influencing the effectiveness of reprimands. *Journal of Applied Behavior Analysis, 15,* 65–83.

Vaughn, S., Bos, C. S., & Schumm, J. S. (1997). *Teaching mainstreamed, diverse, and at-risk students in the general education classroom.* Needham Heights, MA: Allyn & Bacon.

Walberg, H. J. (1990). Productive teaching and instruction: Assessing the knowledge base. *Phi Delta Kappan, 7,* 470–478.

Walker, H. M. (1995). *The acting-out child: Coping with classroom disruption.* Newton, MA: Allyn & Bacon.

Walker, H., Colvin, G., & Ramsey, E. (1995). *Antisocial behavior in schools: Strategies and best practices.* Pacific Grove, CA: Brooks/Cole.

Walker, H. M., & Hops, H. (1993). *The RECESS program for aggressive children.* Seattle, WA: Educational Achievement Systems.

Walker, H. M., Hops, H., & Fiegenbaum, E. (1976). Deviant classroom behavior as a function of combinations of social and token reinforcement and cost contingency. *Behavior Therapy, 7,* 76–88.

Walker, H. M., & Seerson, H. (1990). *Systematic screening for behavior disorders.* Longmont, CO: Sopris West.

Ward, M. J. (1988). *The many facets of self-determination: Transition summary.* Washington, DC: National Information Center for Children and Youth with Handicaps.

Wehby, J. (1994). Issues in the assessment of aggressive behavior. *Preventing School Failure, 38* (3), 24–28.

Wehman, P. (1990). School-to-work: Elements of successful programs. *Teaching Exceptional Children, 23,* 40–43.

Weinner, H. (1969). Conditioning history and the control of human avoidance and escape responding. *Journal of the Experimental Analysis of Behavior, 12,* 1039–1044.

Wesson, C. L., & King, R. P. (1992). The role of curriculum-based measurement in portfolio assessment. *Diagnostique, 18* (1), 27–37.

Wiggins, G. (1991). Standards, not standardization: Evoking quality student work. *Educational Leadership,* 18–25.

Willis, S. (1992). Technology education seen as a new basic. *ASCD Update, 34* (9), 3.

Wilson, E. A. (1996*). The Internet roadmap for educators.* Arlington, VA: Educational Research Service.

Witt, W. C., & Martens, B. K. (1983). Assessing the acceptability of behavioral interventions used in classrooms. *Psychology in the Schools, 20,* 510–517.

Wolf, D., Bixby, J., Glenn, J., & Gardner, H. (1991). To use their minds well: Investigating new forms of student assessment. In G. Grant (Ed.), *Review of research in education* (pp. 35–39). Washington, DC: American Educational Research Association.

Wolf, K. P. (1992). *Informed assessment of students through the classroom literacy portfolio.* Unpublished doctoral dissertation, Stanford University, CA.

Wong, K. L. H., Kauffman, J. M., & Lloyd, J. W. (1991). Choices for integration: Selecting teachers for mainstreaming students with emotional or behavioral disorders. *Intervention in School and Clinic, 27,* 108–115.

Wood, C. L., Nicholson, E. W., Findley, D. G. (1985). *The secondary school principal.* Newton, MA: Allyn & Bacon.

Wood, J. W., & Long, N. J. (1994). *Life-space intervention: Talking with children and youth.* Austin, TX: PRO-ED.

Wynne v. Tufts University (U. S. Ct. App., 1990).

Ysseldyke, J. E., & Algozzine, B. (1990). *Introduction to special education* (2nd ed.). Boston: Houghton Mifflin.

Zeiler, M. D. (1972). Superstitious behavior in children: An experimental analysis. In H. W. Reese (Ed.). *Advances in child development and behavior* (pp. 1–29). New York: Academic Press.

INDEX

Academic restructuring, 112
Academics, program guidelines, 109–110.
    See also Curricula; School curriculum
Achievement, and CBA, 49
Acting-out, crisis development level, 103
Action-impulse mode, appropriateness
    of, 5
Adlerian theory concepts, positive disci-
    pline, 98
Administration, computer programs for,
    58–59
Adult life transition, model program, 121
Aggressive students, management tactics,
    100
Alternative assessments, 45–47
Alternative programs, 115–116
America On-Line (AOL), 58, 59
Anger: student's displacement of, 101;
    tactics for management, 100
Antecedent-behavior-consequence
    (ABC) analysis, taping of, 60
Anxiety, crisis development level, 102
Art, diversity curriculum, 83
Aspects, synchronous collaboration pro-
    gram, 61
Assessment, definition, 45
Attention Deficit Hyperactivity Disorder
    (ADHD), 138
Attention span, and videodiscs, 62
Audiotaped books, 61–62

Authentic performance-based assess-
    ment, 47
Authoring tools, 56
Authoritative control, 97
Avoidance behavior, teachers', 24, 25

"Barter and bribery," mentality, 30
Behavioral interventions, guidelines, 109
Behavioral management, and alternative
    assessment, 46
Behavior-integrative behavior model, 33
Behavior-isolative behavior model, 33
"Big-ticket item," good behavior, 88
Bio-Sci II Video Tool Kit, 56
Bradford Lesson Planner, Windows soft-
    ware, 54
Braille 'n Speak, 62
Bulletin board services (BBS), 59
Business partnerships, employable skills
    programs, 118–119
Bystanders, need for intervention, 22

Capability, skills for development, 98
Career centers, teacher training pro-
    grams, 9
Career counseling, 116
Career Ladder Program (CLP), 122
CAREER, model program, 122–123
Catch 'Em Being Good Program, 86
Cause and effect, teaching, 99

Center for Reinventing Public Education, University of Washington, 112
Charting, CBA, 48
Classroom meetings, 99; categories of, 108; guidelines for, 108
Collaboration, diversity classroom programs, 81
Collaborative classrooms, 103–104
Common Knowledge, synchronous collaboration program, 61
Community-based instruction, 118, 124
Community service, corrective measure, 9
Community video, 60
Competitive Employment through Vocational Experience (CETVE), 123
Compliments, positive discipline, 99
Computer-assisted design (CAD), 63
Computer-assisted instruction (CAI), 54, 63
Computer skill objectives, elementary students, 63–65
Computer software, writing instruction, 55
Computer stations, 65; first to fifth grade program guidelines, 65–66
Conditioning theory, consistency of behavior management, 80
Confinement, 129
Conflict resolution, 104, 105
Conformity, rules as, 30
Consequences, 13; appropriateness of, 137
Consistency, of behavioral programs/techniques, 21, 89, 128, 129, 137
Content-specific feedback, 13
Content validity, of CBA, 49
Contingency, 21–22
Contingency bias, program interference, 26–27
Contingency disorder, behavior/reward, 29
Contingency-shaped conditioning, 89
Contracting, 27, 95, 132, 136
Cooperative learning, 76–77
Coping skills training, 119–120
COPING, crisis intervention model, 104
Corporal punishment, 5, 6, 8, 9

Corrective feedback, 13; guidelines for, 91
Corrective measures, behavioral problems, 9–10
Counseling, at-risk students, 117
Crisis Development Model, 102
Crisis intervention, 102. *See also* Life-space interview
Cultural diversity, 71
Culture, characteristics of, 72
Curricula: alternatives, 115–116; appropriate and functional, 85–96. diversity, example, 81–84. *See also* Academics; Relevance; School curriculum
Curriculum-based assessment (CBA), 48–50
Custodian, helping as reinforcer, 137

Databases, 55
Defensiveness, crisis development level, 102–103
Delayed reinforcement, 90
Detention, 5, 9
Diagnostic asking, 45
Diagnostic listening, 45
Diagnostic looking, 45
Differential reinforcement, 20, 92, 130
The Digital Chisel, 56
Discipline, 5; problems; underlying causes of, 8–10
Discrimination, 73
Disruptive behaviors: factors causing, 4; reasons for, 10, 11; types of, 11. *See also* Misbehavior
Diverse student classroom: assessment methods, 79–80; assignments variety, 78–79; computer use, 77, 81
Diversity curriculum, example, 81–84
Diversity, facets of, 71
Donations, for token economies, 80, 136
Drill and practice skills, computer-assisted, 57

Educational-diagnostic, class meeting, 108
Educational program planning, and alternative assessment, 46
Educational Research Service (ERS), 69

Effective teaching, 86
Emotionally impacted students, 23
"Employability training," 123
Employable skills: community support, 118–119; school-based jobs, 123
Encouragement, definition, 89
Engaging performance-based assessment, 47
Equity-equal access, computers, 67
Escalation, averting, 100
Escape behavior, teachers', 24, 25
Escort, movement restriction, 135, 138
Essay testing, 43
Evocative effects, behavior modification, 31
Exclusion, corrective measure, 10
Expulsion, 6
Eye contact, case illustration, 129–130

"Finders keepers," rewards as, 30
Fines, corrective measure, 9
First to fifth grade: computer skill objectives, 64–65; computer station guidelines, 65–66
Fixed interval schedule, 92
"Flexibility plans," peer mediation, 106
Follow-up/follow along, at-risk students, 120, 122, 123
Freestyle writing, 78–79
Function: aggressive behaviors, 22; corrective feedback, 13
Functional academics, 123

Games, competitive/cooperative, 62
Gang membership: and feelings, 36; and peer mediation, 28
Generalization, urban behavioral programs, 34
Gifted learners, high technology support, 62–63
Goal attainment of, 5
Goal setting: CBA, 49; goal, 76
Good discipline, characteristics of schools with, 15–16
Grading, traditional, 44
Grant writing, token economies support, 136
Guidelines, classroom procedures and rules, 93

Hidden agenda, program interference, 27
Highrisk children, in urban areas, 4
Hill, Paul T., 112
Homework help, internet, 58
"Hubs," learner-centered setting, 76
Hypermedia, 55

Impulse control, lack of, 4
Impulsive action, value of, 29
In-class isolation (ICI), 89
Individualized educational plan (IEP), 48, 58, 138
In-school suspension (ISS), 7
Instant recall, 43, 45
Interactive games, 62
Interactive videodisc, tutorials, 57
Intermittent monitoring, CBA, 48–49
Internet: homework help, 58; resources for teachers, 69

Job-related skill training, 118
Job-seeking training, 119
Job Training and Tryout Model, 120–121

Kindergarten, computer skill objectives, 63–64

Learner-centered setting, 75, 76
Learning characteristics, 45–46
Learning station/center, 65, 77
Letter grades, 44
Level system, freedom restriction, 133, 135; case illustration, 138–139
Life-space interview (LSI), 96, 131. *See also* Crisis intervention
Limitations, acceptance of, 35
Literacy, diversity curriculum, 83
Literature search, CD-ROM, 63
Littleton, CO, 19
Logging in, student, 65

Mainstreaming, 129, 138; case illustration, 131–132, 138–139; with level system, 135
Manuals, computer training, 56
Mathematics, diversity curriculum, 83
MEAL (Model for Employment and Adult Living), model program, 121
Metacognition, and PA, 51

Misbehavior: causes of, 101; and positive discipline, 97; and punishment, 7; reinforcement of, 93. *See also* Disruptive behaviors

Model programs, at-risk students, 120–123

Monitoring, peer mediation progress, 106

Motivation, 33, 113

Movement, behavior altering strategy, 129; case illustration, 131–132

Multicultural education, goals of, 73

Multimedia instruction, 55–56

Multiple choice-testing, 42, 43–44

"Multiple contingencies," 23

National Association of Elementary School Principals (NAESP), 53

National Crisis Prevention Institute, 102

Natural positive reinforcers, 95–96

Negative behavior management techniques, 92

Negative self-concepts, 4

Newsletter, 56

Noncontingent reward systems, 29

Nonreciprocal outcomes, program interference, 27–28

Nonverbal behaviors, 103, 109

Nonviolent crisis prevention, 6–7

North Carolina Computer Standards, elementary students, 63

Oaklawn Elementary School, Charlotte, NC, 88

Objective testing, 43–44

Objects of trade, reinforcers as, 30

Off-task behaviors, reinforcing, 25–26

One-on-one conferencing, and PA, 50

On-line tutors, 58

Open-ended class meeting, 108

Oppositional Defiant Disorder (ODD), 138

Oppositional values, 4

Oral questioning, 43

Out-of-school suspension (OSS), 7

Parker Middle School, Edinboro, PA, 19

Passive-aggressive student, case illustration, 129–130

Pearl, MS, 19

Peer-hitting behaviors, reducing, 26

Peer mediation, 28, 104–106; training guidelines, 105

Peer reinforcement, removal of, 131

Peer tutoring, 77

Performance-based assessment, 47–48

Permissiveness, 97

Peterkin, Robert S., 112

Phi Delta Kappa Commission on Discipline, 15

Physical punishment, at home, 6

Plan to Teach, Macintosh software, 54

Point systems, 133; case illustration, 139–140

Portfolio assessment (PA), 50–51; Project LINCOL'N, 84; scoring of, 51–52

Portfolio, job competencies, 124

Positive discipline, 14, 97, 98

Positive feedback, definition, 89

Positive reinforcement, 137–138

Power Braille, 62

Power struggles, 93

Praise, as reinforcer, 13

Problem-solving: class meeting, 108; skills training, 119–120

Procedural decay, program interference, 25

Program planning, alternative, 117

Project Job, model program, 122

Project LINCOL'N (Living in the New Computer Oriented Learning 'Nvironment), Springfield, IL, 81–82, 84

Punisher, 13

Punishment: effectiveness of, 7–8, 113; as learning, 31

Pupil-teacher conference, 9

"Reactional biography," behavioral methods, 27

Reciprocal/exchange theory, 24

Record keeping, computer programs for, 58

Reinforcement: description of, 137; priming, 140. *See also* Delayed reinforcement; Differential reinforcement; Positive reinforcement

Reinforcers, 12, 13; functional, 36; as objects of trade, 30; and shaping, 92

Relevance: contingencies, 28, 29; curricu-
lum, 14; 85–86; model programs,
123–124
Reliability of behavioral programs, 21
Repertoire-altering effects, behavior
modification, 32
Restitution acts, 132
Restructuring, class situation, 109
Routine contingencies, as coercive, 30
Rule-governed conditioning, 90
Rules, classroom behavior, 94, 104

Safer-school campaigns, 20
Salvaged vs. earned rewards, 29
School curriculum, relevance, 14
School discipline policies, 12
School failure, 41
School-family involvement, 74–75
School-related causes of misbehavior, 11
School store, ticket/token redemption,
87, 136, 140
Schoolwide behavioral management, 102
Science, diversity curriculum, 82
Self-control, reasons for teaching, 14, 15
Self-determination skills training,
117–118
Self-evaluation, 49; freestyle writing, 79;
and PA, 50
Self-expression, and varied assignments,
78
Self-reflection, 49; and group learning,
77; and PA, 50
Self-regulation, 49; motivation, 33, 35;
and PA, 50
Sensitivity training package, 37
Setting limits, 93–94, 102
Shaping, 92–93, 133
Short answer test, 44
Simulation programs, 57
Skills transfer, 31
Small-group discussion, 76
Social inequities, increased awareness of,
5
Social studies, diversity curriculum,
82–83
Social validity, 3
Software, selection of, 68
Special programming, 3
Spreadsheet programs, 55
"Stoplight method," behavior control, 88

Strategic-orientation hints, 94
Student-generative reward systems, 35
Students, rights of, 8
Success building, 128; case illustration,
130–131
Superstitious behaviors, 30
Survey sampling, peer mediation effec-
tiveness, 106
Survival adaptive behaviors, 34, 35
Suspension, 6, 11
Sustained feedback, 13
Synchronous collaboration, 61

Tangibles, good behavior rewards, 90–91
Teacher-directed vs. self-regulatory
learning, 33
Teacher education, cultural diversity, 74
Teacher paging, 58
Teacher-student: conferences, 50, 51;
productivity, 54
Teacher training, at-risk students, 119
Teachers insurance policies, violence, 20
Technological integration: planning,
67–68; purchasing pitfalls, 68
Telecommunications, 59–61
Tension reduction, crisis development
level, 103
Testing, computer programs for, 57–58
Therapeutic teaching style, 114
Tickets/tokens, good behavior, 87
Time-out, 7, 23, 89
Timing, mainstreaming, 132
Token economies, 20, 23, 25, 26, 27,
90–91, 129, 135–136; accountancy,
88; case illustration, 139–140; items
used, 91, 136
Topography: aggressive behaviors, 22;
corrective feedback, 13
Traditional assessment, 41, 42–45
Traditional tests: criticism of, 42; types
of, 43
Training goals: incompatibility with
home goals, 32–33; nongenerality of,
31–33
Training, staff in computer use, 68
Transfer hints, 94
Tutorials, computer-assisted, 57

Undocumented immigrant families, 74,
75

Uniform disciplinary guidelines, use of, 16
Urban environment, 4–5
Urban street behavior, variables of, 20
Urban Superintendents' Association of
    America, 112
Urban Superintendents' Program, Har-
    vard University, 112

Variable schedule rewards, 87, 92
Verbal punishment, 5
Verbal reprimands, 9, 91
Vicarious interference, 24–25
Victims, need for intervention, 22

Videotaping, 60
Vocational and career planning, 115, 116
Vocational assessment, 116, 117
Vocational training, 118

Westside Middle School, Jonesboro, AR,
    19
Word processing, 54
Writing, systematic instruction in, 54
Wynne v. Tufts University, 42

Zero-tolerance policies, 19
"Zone of comfort," 103

About the Editors and Contributors

GREGG BYRUM is a business analyst with NationsBank specializing in the use of computer technology. He has worked for the Public Library of Charlotte–Mecklenburg County (NC), supporting their computer technology, training the staff members, and assisting patrons of the library. He was a K–5th grade technology teacher at Oaklawn Elementary School for Math, Science, and Technology in the Charlotte–Mecklenburg School System. His published articles appear in *The Learning Disabilities Association of Charlotte* and *The Idea Exchange*.

JIM CIOCIOLA is an Assistant Principal at James Martin Middle School in the Charlotte–Mecklenburg Public School System. He has worked with behaviorally and emotionally challenged students since 1973. His articles appear in *The Teacher Magazine*. He is currently president of the North Carolina Council for Children with Behavioral Disorders.

BARRY G. MACCIOMEI is a 20-year instructor for children with behavioral and emotional challenges within the North Carolina Public School System. He holds certification in special education (Behavioral/Emotional Disabilities [BED]), regular education (K–8), and vocational education (K–12). He has served on focus groups and committees promoting effective programming for seriously emotionally challenged youth.

NANCY R. MACCIOMEI is currently an Exceptional Children's Coordinator for Support Programs with the Cabarrus County School System in North Carolina as well as an adjunct professor at the University of North Carolina at Charlotte. She has held principal positions for five years, including Morehead Elemenary and Oaklawn Elementary School for Math, Science, and Technology in the Charlotte–Mecklenburg School System and has been an educator in public schools for

23 years. Her recent books with coeditor Douglas Ruben include *Homebound Teaching: A Handbook for Educators; Readings in Aphasia; Readings in Muscular Dystrophy;* and *Readings in Cerebral Palsy.* Her numerous articles appear in *Teaching Exceptional Children, Classroom Teacher,* and the *Charlotte Observer.* She also has a chapter on "Advances in Special Education Legislation" in *Handbook of Childhood Impulse Disorders and ADHD.*

SUZANNE S. PIAZZOLA is currently chairperson of the Special Education Department at Brookland Cayce High School in South Carolina. She coordinates school-level services for special education students and is a consultant for regular staff, guidance counselors, administrators, and support agencies within the community. She has presented at conferences for Council of Exceptional Children, University of South Carolina, and the Mayor's Committee on Hiring People with Disabilities: "Succeeds" Organization. She is listed among *Who's Who among Students in American Universities and Colleges.*

DOUGLAS H. RUBEN is a private-practice psychologist and national consultant on families and behavioral interventions in schools. He appears coast to coast on television, radio, and infomericals. He is author and coauthor of 42 books and over 100 professional articles. His recent books on education and treatment include *Assessing and Treating Addictive Disorders; Transitions: Handbook of Managed Care; Family Addiction; New Ideas in Therapy; Current Advances in Psychiatric Care; Homebound Teaching; Handbook of Behavioral Interventions; Aging and Drug Abuse; Handbook of Childhood Impulse Disorders and ADHD; Avoidance Syndrome;* and *Treatment of Adult Children of Alcoholics: A Behavioral Approach.* His self-help and practitioner guidebooks of late include *No More Guilt: 10 Steps to Shame-Free Life; Bratbusters: Say Goodbye to Tantrums and Disobedience; One Minutes Secrets to Feeling Great; Your Public Image: Using TV, Radio, and Print Media in Clinical Practice;* and *Writing for Money in Mental Health.*